Deliver

Deliver

Shelle Graves

Copyright July 2015
Unless otherwise indicated in endnotes, all Scripture quotations are taken from the Holy Bible, New Living Translation, copyright © 1996, 2004, 2007, 2013 by Tyndale House Foundation. Used by permission of Tyndale House Publishers, Inc., Carol Stream, Illinois 60188. All rights reserved.
ISBN: 1516862457
ISBN 13: 9781516862450
Library of Congress Control Number: 2015913248
CreateSpace Independent Publishing Platform
North Charleston, South Carolina

Table of Contents

Etc.

§

First, a big thank-you to all the friends and family who made this project possible. Nip, I love you; thank you for Grandma's praying hands. A shout-out to all that are yours. Thank you.

Special thanks to Pastor John Holt of Calvary Church, Jamie Fitt and the ministry of PTOD, Philadelphia Tabernacle of Prayer. There is a special story at the end of this book for you. Thank you all for being faithful and true.

A tremendous heart of gratitude to the love of my life: my husband. Thank you for bearing the weight and burden of this project with me.

I leave a handprint. Not because I'm a theologian, politician, or even an aspiring activist or sociologist, but as a mother, wife, sister, and daughter, I have a legacy and witness to share. As a descendant of slaves, I feel compelled.

To my great-grandfather George Washington Ulysses Grant Thomas, who built houses out of sheer nothingness that still stand today, I say, your struggle was not in vain. God remembers your labor and strain. Thank you for building a place for us to stand.

To my grandfather Worley Samuel Pace, thank you for never giving up or giving in.

In the poetry and storytelling, readers, please note no reference to persons or names is intentional but only accidental and coincidental. All Scripture references and songs are noted in endnotes.

To our three children,

May you go further, may you remember, and may you remind one another that without owning a penny, you have immeasurable wealth inside you.

Love,
Shelle

Dedicated to my beautiful mother

§

EVERY DAY MY FATHER CAME home. He sat in his chair and read his paper. He watched the five o'clock news. He had served in the war. He survived the injustices of being black. He was arrested for standing on a corner. He was simply at the wrong place at the wrong time. He didn't look black: His hair was curly. His skin was fair. He chose to be counted. He stood on the other side of the white line. He was treated unfairly and passed over for his rightful share. But somehow his spirit wasn't bitter. He looked down and shook his head, but he had a peace deep down. Nothing, no words or hate could touch his soul. He called Jesus the Master. Every night I would see him kneel beside his bed and pray. He listened to the most dreadful music I had ever heard with high-pitched ladies' voices and hymns that sounded like howling. Even though he couldn't sing, he joined the choir. He was off pitch, but it didn't matter; he had a song to sing. The Master would hear his voice. As was his custom, my father spoke to everyone he met. He honked the horn at neighbors and talked to waitresses and bank tellers. But it is this one ritual that I never understood till now. Every black man he saw he called Doc. Hey, Doc this. Hey, Doc that. We were annoyed as kids. Why is every one of them a doctor? Didn't he know *mister*?

Now I realize that perhaps this was my father's own way of changing the world one word at a time. He called those black men by a name they may have never, ever been called before. A term of respect. A term of achievement. Honor and dignity. So for the purposes of this book, I am not a school or university or vested with doctoral honors, but I can, for the record, put in print something I believe he deserved.

For the perseverance and labor to survive...
For the sacrifice and service to strive...
For the honor and dignity of choosing marriage...
For your support and tireless encouragement...
For pushing and challenging us to be all we could be...
To go further and be faithful to never forget the God of our Fathers...
I give to you, Daddy, the honorary degree of Doctor.
I honor and thank you as a black man for your presence.
Your influence, your values, your legacy
Your life counted.
Now, I want to give my father, as a representative of all African American men
Another honor. I have never seen it, read it, or heard it.
This day, reader, you are witness to this award.
Black man, descendant of African tribes unknown scattered all over the world.
Brought to this nation in chains on neck, face, arms, and leg irons.
Having endured humiliation, torture, abuse, and neglect.
Having been stripped, whipped, beaten, and bruised.
WE do honor you and award your doctorate degree.
Having not just survived we say thank you,
For bearing the brunt of the savagery
Placed upon your people.
You have worked in the heat of the day with no reward.
You are a great man.
A great warrior.
A timekeeper.
A journeyman.
A world leader.
More than simply a survivor,
You are God's man for the hour.
Thank you; we honor and respect you, black man,
We do call you Doctor.

Soon

Soon-a will be done a-with the troubles of the world
Troubles of the world, troubles of the world
Soon-a will be done a-with the troubles of the world
Goin' home to live with God No more weeping and a-wailing
No more weeping and a-wailing
No more weeping and a-wailing
I'm goin' to live with God
I want t' to meet my mother
I want t' to meet my mother
I want t' to meet my mother
I'm goin' to live with God
I want t' meet my Jesus
I want t' meet my Jesus
I want t' meet my Jesus
I'm goin' to live with God.*

*See endnotes.

NOW

§

WHAT YOU ARE ABOUT TO read is no accident. It is a message for such a time as this. It is both compelling and soul-searching. I believe that the eyes of the Lord are searching throughout the whole earth for those whose hearts are perfect toward Him that He may show himself strong on their behalf.* His eyes also see each and every sparrow that falls. Yes, His eyes even now see the rumblings and tremors of a great shaking in America. Like an earthquake, it is an opening that can bring both opportunity and division. New territories are being established. It is the great racial divide. We are challenged daily. It is front and center in our faces. We must acknowledge it, and yet we must also seek to know the heart and mind of our Lord Jesus in contemplating our response to the questions that arise. Peter exhorts us "to be ready to give an answer for the reason of the hope within you."* We cannot bury our heads in the sands of time and hope that the storms of racial injustices will just blow away. I believe the winds of God's Spirit are indeed removing the dust from the volumes of this great nation's history. Exposing and pressing us to stop and pray and consider not just what in the world is going on, but primarily, what is God up to? Why are we seeing what we are seeing? Why now? How do I reconcile the gospel with the current headlines of our day? Do I just go to church and pray it will all go away? How do I process the stories I hear?

The lens has changed. Literally we are now privy to untold information and footage only made possible through new technology. These images, these are not new. They are just captured. Some seized undercover they reveal for us new evidence. We need to not turn the channel and turn off but tune in to what the Lord is saying to us. To press and hear a perspective so radically different and foreign to our own that it will require a step in a new direction, a step crossing the line into my neighbors' minds. This book is intended to help you do just that. It gives us the waiting room. I am not the doctor, but the doula. I am not presenting a quick do-it-yourself fixer-upper for the plight of a people group. I am praying that the Holy Spirit will reveal in and to you in this book the place to wait and pray, to listen and even say things that are unspoken in our families, churches, or even our own hearts. The empty pages are there for you to reflect and journal where these new boundary lines are being drawn for you. Your conclusions could change the rest of your life.

Please listen to the case and render your own decision of why I believe Jesus is the only answer to the black man and the black man is the answer to American's redemption. This book may bring you to the same opinion or may leave you utterly unconvinced. As an African American, an American, and a descendant of slaves, I question and deeply grapple with my history. I love Jesus and I can honestly say, do not forget my history as well as seeking to walk in fellowship with other believers regardless of their skin color. However, I must admit that as I study history and the hidden grotesque deeds of the past in this nation, my stomach churns, and a deep wound festering and infectious seeps its pus into my heart. For a long time now I have lived with two feet in two worlds: the world of being an American Christian and an African American Christian. I am glad to say that what my great-grandmothers and great-grandfathers saw as a divide, I now possess as a great reconciliation. The fruit may be outwardly reaching, extending hands to another color, but inwardly my soul's soil has been changed. Healing and hope have sprung where only sorrow upon sorrow were felt. I have experienced true bonding to deeper truths and wells of understanding. My hope is that you, as an African American, may also experience great release as the holds of generational condemnation are unshackled from your life.

This narrative is limited as it relates to a people group, African Americans. But it is a story for all of us because it is unlimited, as the tale is retraced throughout all of man's history. Every tribe, nation, people have experienced oppression. Jesus said, "You shall know the truth and the truth shall set you free." So let freedom ring!

This book is essentially comprised of two parts intertwined. It is a discussion removing salvation from the lanes of gospel as we know it and moving it into a narrower scope of salvation as it relates to slavery. Driving the lanes of slavery and its routes as it narrates world and biblical history will give us the perspective, as this term surfaces from the very foundation of God's redemptive plans for man. *Slavery* is an ancient term. This salvation-out-of-slavery paradigm plunges us deep into the Scripture and helps us envision a panoramic view of man and his greatest needs.

When God chose his people, He led them through a multitude of experiences. These experiences serve to give us lessons and establish examples by which we can grow and mature. We find our slave narrative very much hidden in the pages of the Bible. The layout for our discussion includes many forms of prose. Like an opera or cantata, these scenes play images for our eyes to see the interlocking of themes throughout Scripture and its similarities to the whole of the saga of the life and times of the black man and specifically as it relates to God's people. **Author's Note:** For the purpose of our discussion, we will focus on using the term *black man*, as he represents his people, all of his people.

Second, this book is made up of stories. Storytelling was a practice used by slaves to carry their narratives. We will use it as a practical teaching tool so that we may be learning as we are learning. In traditional learning we take the driver's seat in the car. We determine where to stop and how far to go. In storytelling, the story takes the driver's seat in the car and we are in the passenger seat. We don't know where we are going, and we no longer can determine how quickly or slowly we will arrive. We are at the mercy of the story, for good or bad. So ride the waves of storytelling in this book and relax and enjoy. Some of the storytelling does come through song, as songs are the backbone in the African American legacy. It is part of the objective of this book that perhaps you may learn to sing a song other than your own. Whether you know the tunes or not, I encourage you to sing the songs and spirituals in this book aloud. The tune is not as important as your singing. Join your voice with words and heart melodies of stories and God's song over the African American people throughout history. May this book help you find healing as you connect with others and start telling your own story and singing your own songs. You will find that there is a storyteller in all of us. The greatest story ever told is the love story of an infinite God loving a finite people of His own creation.

This entire story process rewrites the scripts in our own minds and links us together as we journey through the narrative. What emerges is a new story for a new day. A new destination. A Promised Land.

Just how do we get there? Through tunnels and bridges as you start to connect to your own life as well as others. Taking the time to go there, start new conversations. As your normal course of day-to-day learned exits of existence reroute through detours and construction zones, this will rekindle old memories. Both good and bad. Please slow down and share them with someone unlike you.

The blessed Promised Land. Where is it, and what is it like? It's a moving picture. You say we already have those. Not movie pictures of scenes choreographed and then replayed perfectly and shot with camera. But a land first of all big enough for all of us, a land where we walk free, not looking over our shoulders, a place without hesitation to hope or where doubts surpass dreams. I believe the Promised Land for the African American is just over the horizon where the sun is due to shine. A land has been purchased. Provisions have been made; it is a prepared place for a prepared people.

God through His Son Jesus Christ has brought us to this mountain. Let us look out not just to our past and see where we have been, but gazing forward look with new vision to see that we are included and destined for a key role in the next move of God on the earth.

*See endnotes.

What If?

§

WHAT IF ALL THE STORIES of every single human who ever lived were written in a book?

Would the book be kept safe on a shelf only for a few eyes?

Would the pages be corrected for historical accuracy and grammar?

What if pictures could tell your story?

Would it be one photograph? Of someone you loved or someone you lost?

And through the course of time, could you, would you with me imagine a gray-haired smiling old man?

See him take the book off the shelf, blow off the dust, and sit down to read your story over and over again with tears in his eyes, with joy in his heart, with shaking hands turning the pages of delight, tragedy, and sorrow, weeping through the torn worded sheets of hearts, homes, and lives shattered?

It is from this book I want to read a little of my own story. As the life that was given to me. But I also hope you find more of your own story as well. Through this progression may your words and pictures get sharper and clearer. Your defining moments seem closer, and the sweetness overtakes the sour.

There are levels to both the telling and the listening. We can tell, but who can listen? "God give us the grace for eyes to see and hearers as well as ears to hear the story, your story through the stories of others." You may have ears but are you the hearer for this story?

Storytelling requires the listener to process information on several tiers simultaneously. My hope is the stories will broaden the definitions, the lines of information coming from the TV and help us to encounter the real raw emotion of history, not just historical "facts." This stone slab is where Jesus comes to meet our needs at this great place of sacrifice. A designated time and place in history. His life for our lives. He gives a new life, a new reality. He is our Redeemer and our Ransom. The Lamb of God who takes away the sin of the world.* I pray that you will learn without intentionally trying to learn and through experience your life may be radically changed to embrace on a living layer the true experiential meaning of salvation through the African American experience.

While seeing and hearing, learning to embrace Jesus and the Bible in the context of African American history gives a real and often harsh and difficult interpretation to digest. Where are the heroes? The happy endings are few and far between. It is a cold and weary world we must enter. But take heart: Jesus willingly enters the story. Is this your time and place to enter as well?

The implications of the stories of the Scripture imprint upon each people group contextualized within that people group's history. Jesus feeding the five thousand meant to my grandmother a promise of provision and trust that I do not experience on a day-to-day level. Yet her telling me that truth in her context enables my faith to grow stronger. Jesus gets bigger and bigger in size to embrace all people. He shines brighter and brighter as I see the darkness of man and his depravity. I love Him more and more, understanding the depth of the chasm between God and man, and man and man, and man and himself. The word pictures through prose or poetry are intended to give you the lens to see a side of the wounds of Christ from a different angle. How deep are the wounds? Just look at history. History defines our wounds as we witness the atrocities of the past and present. Against this backdrop there is no other hope. Not more education or summits or deals can fill the well. It is an eternal miscalculation that computes wrong answers every time.

Jesus is the X factor. Righting the minuses and subtractions, the indifferences and inequalities with truth. X=Truth, which computes to wholeness and rightness (righteousness). An eternal wrong equation is solved by an eternal God. We bow humbly before the Creator of man and the Universe to worship and thank Him for solving the greatest problem on earth. Salvation is beyond beautiful. It is dazzling.

New words for new terms. New language for our new world. Interestingly, growing up I heard big words pronounced not quite correctly. Words were combined, chopped in half, or added to parts of others to express an emotion. *Flustration* is a good example. "It is nothing but sheer *flustration* to try to get through a self-checkout lane in my neighborhood market." It is the words *flustered* + *frustration* = *flustration*. You will not find it in *Merriam-Webster's Dictionary*, but it can be found in the urban dictionary.

On this journey, we will continue to coin words to define and identify expressions in our urban language. I encourage you to do the same. The first is *solvation*. *Solvation* is my term. It is the term defining God's solution to save man. Jesus. Jesus is my salvation and my *solvation*.

Much of our understanding of salvation can focus on the do's and working of things we think we know will please God on a day-to-day basis. However, the Scriptures place heavy emphasis on the totality of the work of Christ. As we travel together through this discussion we must determine whether this totality of the work of Jesus includes all that we are individually as well as sociologically. In a sense, Grandma's Jesus *is* transferable. Not for my salvation, but for my *solvation* and my grandchildren and their grandchildren.

Or is He? Does he save the whole man, the past man, the present man, and the future man? For African American believers, we must back up and hitch the wagon to the faith of our fathers. The past man has been largely forgotten. Things are different and better? Their faith was forged

in the fire of the blacksmiths and in the cotton fields and the praise houses. This Jesus is the answer to our current dilemmas. Jesus is the *forever
solution* for us as a people generationally. We must embrace the totality of
the work of Christ to forge in the present fires the faith we need for the
future.

My greatest expectation is that you will remember and that you will
also forget. Remember your story, your life story as it intertwines all of
your life, your lovelies and *uglies* and loved ones. I pray you will forget the
lulling of the lullabies that have caused you to sleep for so long on your
destiny. Get up and get started walking in the direction of purpose.

Wake up! Shake up! Something is coming. A huge shift is occurring
in America for African Americans. We are at a crossroads and a juncture
from which we may never recover. I am convinced, however, that we are
the generation and we are the people, for we have been given the story
to answer the questions for not just today but tomorrow as well. Look at
your sons, peer into the eyes of your daughters, the questions, the questions are silently, secretly spoken, heard loud and clear in their minds,
Who am I, mommy? Whose am I, daddy? Mommy and Daddy don't know
anymore. Mommy's busy. Daddy was never there. As a people, we are
lost on a sea. Our lives, like a flash in a pan, seem to vanish into vanities.
Simply blank bullets shot into the air. The question remains: Were we
ever here?

We leave no footprints or signposts anymore for those behind us. Ghosts.
Wisps of air, smoke rising from a cigarette. Blown away and shipwrecked by
our own stormy desires. Our boats are seaworthy for only one life. Me. Just
me. A self-consumed once-upon-a-time freed slave who is shackled again by
a relentless master. What's the master's name, you say? Take a drive into the
cities, take a bus after school, ride the subways after work, walk, when the
sun goes down and when the sun comes up. It is summertime.* The babies
have been hushed; indeed the doors have been slammed in their faces. They
are not here with us in this world. Crushed and disfigured, our little ones
still cry, asking why? We are a hot and bothered nation within a nation.

Counting down the count for self-destruction. Five, four, three, two, one fermenting the brew on a stove that is mighty hot.

Out in the distance I see...Like an island we are marooned in the cities. There on the beaches we are surrounded by crystal clear water that we cannot cross. Stuck and stranded we have entertained and eaten. Gorging ourselves we have unstripped and gone naked. Dancing around the fire. So warm and inviting the glow; the rhythmic dance is disarming. We cease to see the daylight or the snakes in the flames. The victims lay waste. Singed by the fire and bit by the snake, no one touches them.

The cities are on fire. The brass heavens are heating up. It is raining. Metals rain from heaven.

Braces, bullets, bars, cages and grates, barbed wires and chains, large iron gates

Metal doors and grilles, metal spoons and plates

A world of heavy objects immovable shapes.

By faith we take up the anvil and hammer and muster the strength to fuel the fire and raise Grandma's hands to beat the hot metal into shape. Strike the metal! Let the sparks fly!

If we don't, those pieces of metal will become heaps of handcuffs for those sitting in our living rooms, eating pizza and hot wings and enjoying just another Redbox* movie.

*See endnotes.

A Man

§

Many, many years ago there was a man.
His skin was as dark as the soil upon which he walked.
Deep and fertile was the valley he ran free.
Barefoot.
From the ridges of the mountains he could cast his vision
Far and wide to see all that he owned and all that he was.
He was a living soil.

Alive. Teeming with life.
He pointed his fingers and traced the clouds in the sky.
His soul rested amid gently sloping hills and gushing waterfalls.

Then from the West came a large vulture bird.
Looking for meat to feed its young.
From far it spotted its prey, springing
Like a herd of horses galloping in glory and freedom
Never missing a stride

Stooping and unsuspecting
The man stopped by the river to take a drink
The giant claws snatched him by the neck
These spears held him motionless
As they flew high in the sky

Past the familiar valleys and mountains
Far over the oceans and beyond any hope of return
The vulture flew faster
Awakened by the chill and wind
The man gripped at his throat
Could not scream nor holler
His was a terror
As he saw hundreds of vultures
Lining the skies

Like tall white ships
Each had a meal's portion
In its talons in the sky

A Balm

There is a balm in Gilead
To make the wounded whole;
There is a balm in Gilead
To heal the sin sick soul.
Sometimes I feel discouraged,
And think my work's in vain,
But then the Holy Spirit
Revives my soul again.
There is a balm in Gilead
to make the wounded whole;
There is a balm in Gilead
to heal the sin sick soul
If you can't preach like Peter,
if you can't pray like Paul,
Just tell the love of Jesus,
and say He died for all.
There is a balm in Gilead
to make the wounded whole;
There is a balm in Gilead
to heal the sin sick soul.*

*See endnotes

A Tree of Life

A tree of life.
From the bark of a tree.
Came the cross.
From the tree under the bark.
Came the ships.
Came the planks of wood.
That we laid upon the sea.
Peering behind the bark of a tree
Came the barking of dogs and
The burning torches in the night looking
From under the bark of the tree came the wagons and wheels
The sticks of wood shooting hot iron
The spinning, tables of wood,
Splitting, spitting hot ovens
Warm beds and blood
The trees hold our bleeding seething
As they still hear our pleadings on the dark side of the moon
The moss helping yet mourning
The cuts on feet pausing to read the path to the North
Under the bark of the tree
Still run the beetles and ants in hollow antiquity
As if the bark of the tree never did see
The deeds of wickedness

Oh bark so rough and callous
So worn and weathered
You protect well inside a secret unseen
'Neath your hard exterior
Your armor clad from birth to cease
A secret sweet runs to the top from deep, deep water
Unlock your mystery hidden
Given
By the Master
For
Out beneath the bark of the tree.
Comes the sap
Sticky warm ready to tap
Its resilient recipe

From the trees of the field
You shall go out with joy and be led forth with peace
the mountains and the hills will break forth before you
there'll be shouts of joy, and all the trees of the field
will clap, will clap their hands
And all the trees of the field will clap their hands
the trees of the field will clap their hands
the trees of the field will clap their hands
While you go out with joy!*

Oh sing all you trees of the South!
Clap your hands trees of the North!
Swaying in spirit, Song trees East and West!
The curse has been lifted, now offer your sap its story and all
Peel off your skin and reveal the moist fresh meat of wood
To be laid upon the hearth
May you ignite the greatest fire in heaven and on earth
Burn, burn, burn plumes of smoke

Leaving only charred black wood ashes and living coals of fire.
From these coals take the tongs and fire upon the tongue
Woe am I for I am undone and I dwell among a people of unclean
lips.*
Nevertheless...
From the bark of the tree.

*See endnotes.

For Aldonia and Artellia

§

I sing because I'm happy I sing because I'm free
Oh His eye is on the sparrow and I know He watches me
Oh His eye is on the sparrow and I know He watches me
Why should I be discouraged and why should the shadows come?
Why should my heart be lonely and long for heaven and home?
When Jesus is my portion, a constant friend is He,
His eye is on the sparrow and I know He watches me.
His eye is on the sparrow and I know He watches me.

I sing because I'm happy;
I sing because I'm free;
His eye is on the sparrow
and I know He watches me.

Let not your heart be troubled; these tender words I hear;
And resting on his goodness I lose my doubts and fears;
For by the path He leadeth but one step I may see;
His eye is on the sparrow and I know He watches me.
His eye is on the sparrow and I know He watches me.

I sing because I'm happy;
I sing because I'm free;
His eye is on the sparrow
and I know He watches me.

Whenever I am tempted; whenever clouds arise;
When songs give place to sighing; when hope within me dies;
I draw the closer to Him; from care He sets me free;
His eye is on the sparrow and I know He watches me.
His eye is on the sparrow and I know He watches me.

I sing because I'm happy;
I sing because I'm free;
His eye is on the sparrow
and I know He watches me...*

*See endnotes.

The Story of Sassy

§

WEARING A YELLOW DRESS, SASSY was the last one to the car every Sunday morning.

"Good morning, child. "Lord have mercy you so late you couldn't beat a snake, if you was racin' for a mile."

"Grandma, what does that mean?"

"What does that mean? It don't mean a thing. Just means you late and always late. It seems you get later by the minute and you fittin' to make all of us late at the same time."

Sassy let out a pout and a sigh. The heavy blue Oldsmobile door creaked as it closed. It was so heavy Sassy was sure her leg would be cut off if she didn't move it fast enough. Terrified of the thought of living without her leg she moved over closer to her brother.

"Move over," he mumbled, giving her a shove back to the door.

"I done," she said.

Slow and steady the car hummed through the trees down the path.

It was their day out. To come out from beneath the miles of woods that stood between them and the world. She was glad to breathe new air and see fresh faces even if it meant settin' through Sunday school. Grandpa donned a white suit and Grandma clutched her Bible. It was bigger than her pocketbook. Grandma would be givin' money to the church and to her to give as well. She thought about slippin' the green dollar bill into her coat pockets instead of the offering plate. *I wonder if to hell I would go.* They was goin' somewhere and nowhere at the same time.

Feeling sad and slow, she didn't know why; she looked out the window for something, anything, new to see. She was glad to leave and grateful to return to the quiet orchards and tobacco plants. Sitting with her back to the fire, she ate grandma's biscuits and cheese for lunch. She dared not eat the salt meat that came from the dark room near the open fireplace. It was salty and tough to chew, and the taste stayed on her tongue for hours. She sneaked the piece of meat off her plate and into her pocket. After lunch she went outside to play with the dogs and feed them her scraps. Although they wasn't the playin' type. They were scrawny and skinny, covered with ticks bulging and ready to burst from all their wild eatin'.

Sassy sat awhile as the dogs argued over the last bits of meat. She would not touch them. Looking at the well with its cover, the clothesline, the red tractor, Grandpa's little house, and the tobacco fields; it had all stayed the same even when she left. She got up, walked the path to the outhouse, still there even though no one used it. She decided she would talk to the pigs. She had refused to love them, to care or feel attached because she knew now what she didn't before. After her feeding and loving them fat they would end up hanging in the room next to the fire. They were to be the next salted pork. The pigs grunted. She *humpf*ed and started to walk. She would only walk so far. She was too scared to go beyond the furthest point she had walked before. Why wouldn't she walk on?

Not sure. Nearly every day she only walked to the edge of the tree line. Grandpa waved and yelled something. She could see they were fittin' to go fishin'. Yuck! Dinner would be fried fish, which she didn't mind so much as the eels. The dogs would be mighty happy to lap up all the parts as the fish were dressed. Fish heads and eyes gobbled up in a hurry. Suddenly she longed for the fire. She ran her familiar path, the door creaked and did its customary slam. Standing at the sink, Grandma was still cleanin' up behind lunch. The floors sung as her heavy body walked across the floor. Her hips swung left then right. Her head was botherin' her.

"Sassy, go get me a BC and a Coca-Cola."

"Yes ma'am."

She ran back to the kitchen as she heard Grandma fall near the sofa. She was a heavy woman bearing the weight of the world on her shoulders. "Sassy! Come here and help me get up." She was inches from completely lying on the floor clutching the edge of the brown couch, she was wedged between the coffee table and the settee. The black coal stove was hot to the touch and sat right next to the sofa. It was on full blast and the room was hot. Sassy set the BC and Coca-Cola down as she tried to get Grandma set right. She unlocked the front door so air could come in. "Sit here awhile, Grandma."

Sassy ran outside and sat under a peach tree. There on the ground were peaches firm and ripe. She bit into one. It was not sweet; she had bitten into a worm. This was her favorite place to sit. Seeing the fields from the top of the hill, fields as far as the eye could see. The dirt road separated from the path in the woods and traveled down the curve. To the right it passed her. *Maybe I could walk this way, follow this path*, Sassy thought fleetingly as she threw the peach over the steep cliff.

They were rich in land and yet so desperately poor. They lived on the brink of extinction and disaster. No one to catch them if they fell. All could be lost within an instant. Each breath they took they knew it was given. Dependent upon a mercy and grace that ran deep as the soul's soil. Reckless, humans plowing and sowing, reaping maybe this season. Maybe not making it another. A life still as a windowpane. Clear and faultless. Ready for its shattering. By the hands of another or from within themselves.

A life.

Sassy picked up another peach and bit again.

Like Snowflakes in a Water Globe

§

There in midair walking the tightrope
Was the black man and his family
Empty chairs at the struggling kitchen table
Broken dishes
The screen door slams shut
In and out
Castaways or
Survivors
Shipwrecked
Nonetheless persons in a world-turned-upside-down snow globe
At the whim or desire to be whimsical
Nevertheless the snow blows through the water
Tilting...all sits right-side-up once more
till the call comes to be tossed

Consider Sassy

§

LIFE AS STILL AS A windowpane. There is a thin frame that holds this fragile world together. Looking through her eyes we can experience a stillness and sense a distant tension that something is not right.

A sharp edge is right around the corner. The axis is just off center, causing a shift where everything and anything can slide off the table at any moment. Nothing is permanent. Nothing is sure. Therefore she breathes in shallow sips of air. Waiting almost expecting the next dreaded thing. Nothing is happening and yet everything is happening; Sassy lives looking into the snow globe. She cannot define it but it is in the air she breathes. She has been steeped like a cup of tea with an inward unease and apprehension. From this story there are thoughts and lessons that we can learn from Sassy that will help to frame and give us the boundaries to relate and empathize with the African American experience. Though it is not dramatic or even that interesting, its tale helps us identify themes and circles of black life history.

As a people, WE are folks of Broken Circles and disconnectedness. Like Sassy we sense the distance as Sassy experienced in her:

1. Emotions: She is unable to account for her reasoning.
2. Animals: She has learned to distance herself from attachments and feelings.
3. Self: She is alone though surrounded by others.
4. Brother: He is present but not necessarily desiring her company, companionship or closeness.

5. Grandfather: Physical distance represents a figure she sees but does not relate to.
6. Grandmother: Their relationship consists of do's and don'ts.
7. Land itself not enjoying the sweetness: Land produces an uncertainty of harvest. This anxiety is felt.

There on the farm in her short existence there is a mist of clouds that make all of life seem detached and filled with tentativeness. A general uncertainty pervades the air. Being confined to shallow breathing, the African American experience is transient and unpredictable. Easily disrupted and without any hedges of protection for future concerns, it is riddled with instability.

Every color in the story is in basic primary color schemes. There are no pastels or gentle mixtures. Basic necessities, no frill or lace depicts the African American experience as well. Limited if any choice at all is the depiction. Pervading thankfulness is often expressed to have what you had because you knew so many others who were less fortunate. There is no luxury of choosing what colors you wanted; life for many is simply not to die. Survival is a day-by-day journey. The basic color schemes are:

1. Yellow dress
2. Blue car
3. White suit
4. Red tractor
5. Brown couch
6. Black stove

Sassy lived with limits and lines, strange boundaries seen and unseen. Some of these limits were mental. Some physical. Others imaginary and yet some more real than she could have ever imagined. We see this depicted in the story as:

1. Sunday: the only day out
2. Money: given to give away

3. Dogs: to feed, not to play with
4. Pigs: to feed, not to love
5. Walks: not to be explored but set
6. Relationships: conversations that are instructive and scolding, directives but not affirming
7. Alone yet within a context of family
8. The farm and its survival not spoken of, yet of primary importance

This heavy weight upon life is almost impossible to define. It would be like trying to run free in a field where you knew grenades were planted. Every moment of every day could potentially explode by the greater world system in which you lived. Something as simple as going to the store or running an errand could end your life. *Fear is a living person who walks the hallways and drives the lanes of the African American runway from coast to coast of these United States.* Fear has been planted deep in the soil of the black man's soul.

So let us enter the conversation of African American history by moving out of our modern thinking into the story of Sassy, in which life is defined by purpose only, not relationships.

The purpose of the pig is to be eaten, to provide food. The purpose of the dogs: for hunting and security. They were not friendly. Neither were they cared for or cuddled. The relationships were not nurtured. A life was measured in what it could or could not produce. Life could be extinguished or merely thrown off a cliff as meaningless as a piece of unwanted fruit. As numerous as the fruit, black lives were seen as an inexhaustible supply of fuel to fire the slave machinery. Replaceable and having little value. These attitudes still infiltrate our thinking as others' viewpoints as well as our own. We are a people whose mirrored image is marred and disfigured.

Our only hope is to exchange our mirrors for windowpanes. Hearts that are clear before a Savior.

Empty Boxes

Ice crystals falling
Cold frozen fingers are blue
Never not warm
Hungry
Skinny bony spine poking out just above the collar
Raggedy rough burlap dress
Not enough to cover
Shoeless feet
Walking the road alone
Severed from those I love
Fears fall like rain
Dressed and covered still I feel naked and ashamed
Inward pieces
Fragmented
Disfigured
The pieces of my puzzle
Perplex my mind
Torment my soul
I long to belong
I wish to be held
I desire to be wanted
To sit and retell the stories
And open the memoir trunk

To pass down the riches
To bring out the bank statements of inheritance
But as I sit still the moving van arrives
They arrived early I am mournful to discover
All my boxes are empty
Empty boxes
Already opened by marauding pirates
For I have been pillaged all along the way
Raped
Looted
Stolen from
Outwitted
Hoodwinked
Bamboozled
By man
Outside by law
There's nothing to unpack
So I just stand here in the street
Am I nobody? With nothing at all?

The Tree out on the Street

§

My black hands are soiled, stained, and bruised from the gory battle of self-destruction
I stand on the corners pumping drugs in my arms
Smoking my brains to the sky
Green, green grass
Hoping to get higher than the hatred I feel inside
Birthed in iniquity, sold upon my birth to inequality
To a master cruel and unrelenting
He says I am cursed
Cursed beyond my mind's imagination
Cursed from the God of the Bible
And curse by a verse*
He taunts me and sings
"What can make me White as snow?"*
This black-brown skin is covered by the soil
And by the lashing of its soul will it never recover
Vulnerability
Courage
Nurture
Wealth
Like a kite without a string
Will the black-face man ever stop floating?
Higher and higher without any strings

He flies upon the air of injustices
Winds of turmoil and restlessness
Lifting him into the land not of freedom nor promise
But *lostness*, ever higher and deeper downward in cycles
On crumbled cement steps of man's depravity
Be careful you'll fall
Forever falling
Being tossed by the sea
He's thrown down the depths of a drain

Black man
Climb out upon the limbs
Like arms and oars of ships standing
As legs of a resurrected tree
Climb higher than your soul-claimed corner
And your feats of pleasure
Ruse rouse ruff your self
Climb greater to see that
This tree from the sea yet rises
A tree of bodies lost in the sea
Join in your song as the sea
Sings
Cries
Weeps
Mourns
A storm is a brewin'. Here far out upon the seas
The tree rocking like an empty chair by a standing facing backward
Young crazy frenzied child
Rocking faster back and forth, it's gonna tip over
Never slower rocking
Violently. Get out of the car. Put your hands up. You have the right to.
Really? Maybe not.
Hands behind your back.

The tree out upon the sea.
Jesus walks.
Speaks.
Still.
Peace.

See endnotes.

A Confession on the Circumstantial Evidence of Self-Destruction

§

I have been taught to hate myself.
To dislike my skin
The lighter the better
Relieved when heard
"It's OK, you're not that dark"
To feel ashamed of my past
To regret my children's destined path
To fear the future
Be embarrassed
To feel removed
Out of place
Not at home
Like a dark cloud
Rising every day
Whether sunny or raining
It still stays in place
Gloom over my past
Gloom over today
It will be cast over me whatever way I take
So why not self-destruct

Why not hate
Being tied to the stake
Why not set on fire
To be free from my own chicken wire

The Testimony of a Signature

§

INVITED TO A GALA EVENT commemorating the accomplishments of black community activists, the individuals stood in line. They were asked to sign and waited one by one. They understood the significance of their signature. They signed remembering. Their very presence was heralded by a clarion call; they had come out of the woodwork to bear witness. To their own deeds, to their struggles, and to their victories. Many of these elders bore the scars of their journey. They had walked and talked with the greats of our most recent history. Their signatures gave testimony to the fact that they had not only survived, but they were overcomers. It didn't matter how long they waited and what type of paper, they would leave witness.

Stolen and deposited into a land not their own, the African American signature is a symbol. A symbol of dignity and respect. It states, I am not an animal. I am a human being. I can be acknowledged and will be considered for all rights and legal protection as a legitimate-born citizen.

The signature makes a statement. The signature tells a story. It says, I am here. My life matters.

Like a Parade

§

Like a parade they came. Displayed like peacocks.
All shapes and sizes
Suits colors and capes
tight dresses elegant
Hats amid long flowing coats like drapes
Some were proud in their gait
Some slow in intentional
Some swaggering
Some lagging
Some leaning on a staff
Wrinkled worn foreheads
Curly permed and dreaded hair
Wild frayed split at the ends
Gray black brown and red
Bushy straight short and long
Heavy weights in a culture important to someone
These no longer shackled but now dressed to kill
Each made a statement a step in pride I have walked the earth
and passed time
My brothers and sisters I have a voice for I know I am somebody
I will wait in line to say my name because I can
Because I am who I am and nobody else
I say it clearly in rhythm. I say it loud not to be misunderstood

"I am Sarah Johnson"
"I am Mattie Davies"
"My name is..."
All were sons and daughters of former slaves
Dressed in furs and long white coats
Shades of dark and butter browns
Alligator shoes, on top cowboy hats off
I don't think so, not tonight
They were proud
They stood in line waiting to sign
In...finally
They had been called to a gala event to commemorate
Austerity and action
To mark accomplishment and progress
With each face I felt enriched and empowered
I claim them as my family
This is my tribe
The whole lot of them even the man seven feet tall
They are afro Americans
These are my people.
Yes I belong with them and though we feel we belong nowhere
We belong to each other
Standing in circles with chains still littering the floor
We still standing in wonder and awe of our history
We've been through...How we still standin'...Lord only knows
He's been deliverin' us for hundreds of years
He knows all our names
We've just never signed them before
Didn't know how
Didn't know we could
Never stood in lines
Never been invited
Never was important

Never made a memory on purpose
Or choose to
Save a date
All was given to try to forget
Everything
That ever happened. O me and mine and all my kind.*
"In this land was made for you and me.*"

We are a people.
WE are a tribe
So sign

*See endnotes.

Your Sign in the Sky

§

If you are reading this book, please sign here

_____

Your signature

SIGN, IN RECOGNITION THAT YOU are not a mistake. Your life has eternal purpose. Your African American history has beauty and meaning and great worth and significance to the world in which you live. Your story is unique and its value is incomparable. As an African American you possess great wealth. God has ordained your life for this time in history. In His equation of the universe, your life matters.

The Vision of Heaven

§

AND HE CAME AND TOOK the book out of the right hand of Him who sat on the throne. When He had taken the book, the four living creatures and the twenty-four elders fell down before the Lamb, each one holding a harp and golden bowls full of incense, which are the prayers of the saints. And they sang a new song, saying, "Worthy are You to take the book and to break its seals; for You were slain, and purchased for God with Your blood men from every tribe and tongue and people and nation...

> Worthy are You to take the book and to break its seals; for You were slain, and purchased for God with Your blood men from every tribe and tongue and people and nation...
> For You were slain, and purchased for God with Your blood men from every tribe and tongue and people and nation...
> And purchased for God with Your blood men from every tribe and tongue and people and nation...
> Men from every tribe and tongue and people and nation...
> Every tribe and tongue and people and nation...
> Let us fall down and worship...
> Can you hear this song?
> Let us sing, "Worthy are You to take the book and to break its seals; for You were slain, and purchased for God with Your blood men from every tribe and tongue and people and nation...*

*See endnotes.

A Witness to the Bonfire

∫

DRIVING HOME ONE NIGHT FROM my high school football game, I saw a glow and smoke rising over a steep cliff. Being nosy, I tried to look but could not get a clear view. So I turned my car around and from my vantage point could see a gathering. White sheets with pointed hats were circling a bonfire. It was a terrifying sight. In some ways I wished I had never looked. That picture broke the mirage of all I had experienced at the football game as a member of this and friends with them. It also shattered my very thin wall of reality. I had seen something. I could detour the road but these were my neighbors, the parents of my classmates or my classmates themselves. Just who were behind the masks I would never know. Secrets now seen, I lived in the shadows of a deep dark monster that covered its face and warmed itself by a fire.

Hell on a Horse: The KKK

§

Hoofs pounding the streets
They came hooded on horseback
Determined to keep their order
and world intact
They rode incognito under cover of darkness
Cowards concealed in white sheets
Coming to cover alive
To steal life
Hell hounds on horseback
Monstrous mirages figures of doom
Corpses singing hymns of glory
Bearing crosses set on fire
Their mere shadows terrorize
Stop the beating heart with fear
Lynch mobs, hangings, torturing, maiming, decapitating
Called and summoned by a creed they claimed as Christ's
To resist, to flog, and restrain those they disdain
No dogs
No Negroes
No Mexicans
No Jews
Colored only served out back

The henchmen waiting and debating
Where shall we hang him?
Never mind just drown him
Dump him
Underneath the icy frozen water
Lies, so many lies
The watery casket opens and swallows

A branch from the tree of life
Raises over the oceans
"Pharaoh's chariots and his army he has hurled into the sea. The best of
Pharaoh's officers are drowned in the Red Sea. The deep waters have cov-
ered them; they sank to the depths like a stone."*
Yet a Lifeless body submerged in suffering beneath
In the belly of the depths of the deep
Here THE TRUTH speak, "Lazarus, come forth."*

"But Lord he stinks."*
The whole reeking history stinks of putrid death.
A cold hand grabs our chin to make us look at the tomb.
A blanket of evil reserved for the darkest of cold nights.
No light. Closed. The tomb sealed. Ever wounds seeping serious memory.
There is no hope. There is no direction. There is no one who can speak to
this sepulchre of endless
Recollections of fears and agony. Terrors in the night. Sleepless night-
mares these costumed cruel
Creatures dance and act. Practicing in twilight. Performing deforming
before daybreak.
Godless men with pointed hats bring their wicked bags of tricks to vanish
baby cradles. Bare bassinets.
Devoid of mercy
Absent of conscious

Hollow-souled logs hoisted upon the flames. Hotter still hotter. Hot as hell itself.
Stagnant winds fan the rage.
Tongues on fires of Babel. Speaking walls of hatred, oppression, racism
Killer speeches.
Raising shameless stairways of supremacy to their heaven.
A world without_____.

"Lord if only…"*
Zzzzzzzzzzzzzzzzzzzzzzz
Sleep. Lazarus. Sleep.
Jesus weeps.*

"Roll away the stone."*
The resurrection speaks.
"I am the resurrection."*

"Lazarus, Come forth."*
In white sheets. Unwrap him. "Remove the grave clothes."*
For he is alive.

*See endnotes.

Let Us Gather

Shall we gather at the river,
where bright angel feet have trod,
with its crystal tide forever
flowing by the throne of God?
Refrain:
Yes, we'll gather at the river,
the beautiful, the beautiful river;
Gather with the saints at the river
that flows by the throne of God.

On the margin of the river,
washing up its silver spray,
we will talk and worship ever,
all the happy golden day.

Refrain:
Yes, we'll gather at the river,
the beautiful, the beautiful river;
Gather with the saints at the river
that flows by the throne of God.

Ere we reach the shining river,
Lay we every burden down;

Grace our spirits will deliver,
and provide a robe and crown.

Refrain:
Yes, we'll gather at the river,
the beautiful, the beautiful river;
Gather with the saints at the river
that flows by the throne of God.

At the smiling of the river,
Mirror of the Savior's face,
Saints, whom death will never sever,
lift their songs of saving grace.

Refrain:
Yes, we'll gather at the river,
the beautiful, the beautiful river;
Gather with the saints at the river
that flows by the throne of God.

Soon we'll reach the silver river,
Soon our pilgrimage will cease;
soon our happy hearts will quiver
with the melody of peace.

Refrain:
Yes, we'll gather at the river,
the beautiful, the beautiful river;
Gather with the saints at the river
that flows by the throne of God.*

*See endnotes.

A Mother's Lament

§

From her eyes pour the waters to baptize his soul to rid him of this torturous rant

That he doesn't fit neither can ever belong

Not coveted just loathed beyond hated reviled

Pull back my son from your suicidal syringe that feeds you and intoxicates and numbs you

Within

What can I say what can I do

I tried my best to keep you inside where we eat and sleep in peace beside a warm open stove

But the time came you had to leave my door and stand on the porch of another's floor

Not asking for anything but opportunity to leave mama

"There's no place for me. No one answers their door, they see me comin' and pull their blinds,

"Shut the doors. Why didn't you tell me I had no place to go?"

Reaching behind her, Mama pulls up a sack, a legacy, a history of the stories of coming back.

I thought things were different. Seemed things had changed. I didn't realize you just got bigger

But the chains remained the same.

Lazarus Is Arising...

I hear Lazarus stirrin' in his grave
They bound him and laid him
Deep within and veiled
But there's a crowd rushing
Quickly to the outskirts of town
Folks sayin' crazy things
Like a dead man comin' out
Comin' out of his grave

I see Lazarus he's a standin'
There beyond the rock rolled away
Can't see him clearly 'cause there's
An unveiling to be made
But I can't believe what I'm seein'
First the stone rolled away
Then a dead man
A sure enough bonafide miracle
Is standin' here today

Do you see him?
Can you hear him?
He may be snorin' on your couch
As good as a dead man given up on life

Wrapped in impossibilities, heartaches, and strife
Debtor to the debt
Bloodied by the self-stoning
He's a spaced-out selfish junkie
Father to not a few
He appears washed up and forgotten
Groaning and smelling
Coughing and crumbling one-dollar bills together to pay for tomorrow

Stop your crying
You hear me!
No more weeping...
Jesus is on the way...

Tears of Our Mothers

§

And we went down to the river to pray*
Celebrating and rejoicing the good ole way
Oh sisters lets go down

Way down into the reeds we laid him
Knowing full well if not they will enslave him
His mother worried and distraught
Counted the cost and figured his lot
Up river he would go

A mark given perhaps to note his birth
But why threaten his chance of wealth
Born of new lineage born a new son
She kissed him good-bye
As a mother to her son

Step back from the water
Step back from the shore
Where does the water lead?
Where does the stream empty forth?

From the reeds and the mud
From the deeds of ruthless ones

She sent him up
But he went down for his destiny to be found

Up from the river
Crying is the babe
Born from the womb of her waters
Go fetch a handmaid

Laid in a basket
As a tomb like a boat
His journey uncertain
By his mother's faith
He flowed
Seized by separation
By an edict and decree
This Moses fellow
This one boy survivor
Would lead His people
By His rod to be freed

So search and see

Was he not certain for death by ruling?
Black boys before birth
Are threatened
Before they set foot on earth our midwives arrive to warn
And carry to the shores
You must ride rivers flowing from the tears of your mothers
The basket set afloat to journey
Apart we send them
Runaway slaves
Send them away you can no longer stay
Your life is threatened by verdict and edict

A sentence to be
Go now part the seas
Beside the reeds
Awaits your calling

*See endnotes.

Down in the River

As I went down in the river to pray
Studying about that good old way
And who shall wear the starry crown
Good Lord, show me the way
O sisters let's go down
Let's go down, come on down
O sisters let's go down
Down in the river to pray
As I went down in the river to pray
Studying about that good old way
And who shall wear the robe and crown
Good Lord, show me the way
O brothers let's go down
Let's go down, come on down
Come on brothers let's go down
Down in the river to pray
As I went down in the river to pray
Studying about that good old way
And who shall wear the starry crown
Good Lord, show me the way
O fathers let's go down
Let's go down, come on down
O fathers let's go down

Down in the river to pray
As I went down in the river to pray
Studying about that good old way
And who shall wear the robe and crown
Good Lord, show me the way
O mothers let's go down, come on down
Don't you want to go down
Come on mothers let's go down
Down in the river to pray
As I went down in the river to pray*

*See endnotes.

The MAN speaks

§

From the heights above the man lets out his moan
I hear voices and music up here in the sky
Stories and stories
Tales upon tales
Testimonies and prayers
Talks and songs
Conversations
Whirlwinds of arguments spinning
Will anybody listen?
Will anybody tell?
Expose erase eradicate the lies and missed fortunes
Will anyone stop at the gate?
And say

THE SKY IS FALLING, I say
THE SKY IS FALLING

All the words are coming down
Like pitter-patter pitter-patter on the gutters
But they are b-b-b-bombs of discolored revelations
What is white?
What is black?
I am stuttering I can't quite say it

But listen for yourself
Why is it
Now
Here
That we have so much, no, so little to say?

Stone Trippin'

Tripping over beer cans
Street lights flickering
Green-eyed cameras watchin' us go and come
With our sagging and nagging
Uneven concrete sidewalks
Gates and grates iron fences
Rocks...shots fired. Minutes later, sirens blarin'
Sneakers hanging on telephone lines' graffiti
Plastic palm trees planted leftovers spread out
Dogs barking earlier and earlier and later and later
Music with too many beats
Cats roamin' smells smokes yells doors slammin' cursin'
Freely frequenting peein'
There I saw him
Walking barefoot through his treeless park
Not scared of the glassed grass
Takin' a break from play
He sweeps the curb with his worn out broom
Tired of cleanin' and cheatin'
Goin' nowhere and doin' nothin'
Nothin's movin'
All is still no wind at all
No one's comin' no one's leavin'

All is still, no wind at all
This lion this warrior this nobody but everybody's child
I picked him up and took him home.

Boomerang

This once a child now a man grew up and tried to sail off the island
We all stood and gave witness
Shook hands and patted ourselves on the back
We weren't perfect but thought we had done enough
Sacrificed enough
Preached enough
We filled his sack with silver cups and grain
His boat filled with faith and salted fishes
Hopeful that he would return with the ships and supplies
To end our desertion
Our famine and demise
We bid him go
We gave him all we had and then some more
Beyond broke we had spent all of yesterday's, today's, and tomorrow's paychecks
To get just a token
A one of us in a world far, far away
He was leavin' the island we were proud to say

Not first to know we refused to listen to hear
The stories they had to be lies
I saw him leave, I saw it for myself
What do you mean his body washed up on shore?

The cross-current they say the tide was too strong
His boat not sturdy the wood porous
Like a sponge absorbed the waters of the sea
It did not float at all just sank to the bottom
The clothes on his body served like a mast on a skipper
And brought his island-stuck soul back to the stranded crowd by the sea
Tasered by the ocean
Motionless he lay facedown
Handcuffed by futility
His locks cut
He washed up in defeat
Beached
His angry forehead propped up on the porch of his doubly purchased oceanfront sand castle property
First by birth now by confinement no auction this time the gavel slams sold!
As the waves hit the shore
We stood in a circle around him
Fanning the flames
Will his clothes ever dry from the storms and beating inside?
Come now, my sisters, let us sing sweetly over him to comfort as his conscience does rise.
To keep his mind inside him for to the death of his dreams he does awake.

Still

Heavy from the water
The pants sag
They droop
Exposing and negating with every step
The legacy of where we've been and who we are
It's a statement rooted in hopelessness
Can you blame him?
I don't know who I am
I don't know where I am going
I have not comprehended who I am in my present reality
Therefore look at me
Walking back and forth on this damn island
My pants hanging
Belt tied around my knees
My underwear to see
Aiming to please nobody not even me
I'm strung stung and forsaken of a popular cult
Who's gone naked
So look upon my backside and see
THAT I DON'T EVEN CARE WHAT I LEFT BEHIND ME
Cause I don't look at what's behind just forward
Not even darin' to turn around and realize
Who might be following me?

Well if you for one moment could believe
That you can't go forward till the past you see
We was naked
Had no legacy
No name
Nobody following us
But now my brother you want to take us back
To exposing and shaming and belts around our knees
Who says turn it down
WE do
We all do
All your mothers and fathers and greats and grands
We is de ones standin' behind you
Lookin' at your hind parts
Your last mile
Turn around and smile
We got your back
We're clothing you
In the rags
They're not torn 'cause they just cast lots for this suit
We be wrappin' and spinnin' you in new threads that cover all of
you
Every last inch of you we done covered in prayer
Dragged through the fire
And plead by the blood
Heaved your body out of the sea
You are walkin' cause we sagged by force
But now we stand and say no more
Stand up, my brother
Pull up your pants
Let me help you with your jacket
Its designer-tailored fit a double-breasted mantle for you to
take beyond where it's been tested

Fit to fit only you and your perspective
Get up, stand straight, head up, shoulders back
You've got somewhere to get goin'
The world is the stage waiting for you to release my black-brown brother
A heavenly message!
We are getting off this island.

All There Is

You can't convince me no matter how hard you try
To be satisfied with
My extra seated foldaway van,
My leather suit or my black and red Jordan's
You can't make me sit down and ask for no more
Than a 52-inch Blu-ray television and pink beats
Keyless entry and a pew by stained-glass
So what I have a walk-in closet and an extra stove burner
I can look out and see a yard in front and a fence out back
I come and go as I please
Lite soy vanilla lattes
Vaca by the beach
Is that where I'm destined to bask in the glory of my great
grandmothers gone gory life story
Tones from the underbelly of the world's greed come to sur-
face while I try to sit and be content
I solace and attempt to be silent
But, lo, something is movin' in me, I hear a grim groan and try to
ignore and strive
To live good to absorb all of this good given to be the American
dream
But as I take a seat and simmer I hear her
Songs, her wailings and travailing prayers at midnight

Frights at night
Draping curtains for her see-through house pitched by the swamp
Seclusion on segregation's avenue with a stand in the corner holdin'
Umbrellas kept for all these years for the tears rainin' down on the whole lot of them
Them-the groves of trees sprouted by the busy boulevard, not planted just grown up from tossed seed
I look up at the bright blue sky with the white pillowy clouds and say
Grandma, it's still there
Your same sun
Your same stars
Your same moon
Your same scars
It's me, I am a subject of change
Not submitted to chains
Or am I?

I won't forget!
I won't let me myzelf or I go to sleep!
I'll keep myself awake!
But it's pulling me in day after day this way, the whole world says, its shouts louder everywhere I go
Buy it sleep eat and taste it try this ties like anchors to my soul
I'm sold once again auctioned off this
time to vain meaningless gods who are good for nothing but enslaving to debt and debtors
Rubberstamping generations, ditto and copies, Xeroxed stereotypical episodes on full screen
Full definition without color or colors blended ever-so-blended into nothing more than backdrops for someone else's dreams

Shade me in colors not gray and faded

With its cries it tries to get me to forget there ever was a struggle or a stripe upon your back

This slouchy bog holds me in quicksand to only do what's been done and only go as far as has been gotten, don't go no further

Don't think just react don't read just listen don't ever be silent for just one minute

Keep dancin' and tweetin' stay in a trance mind clouded strung out on lines of ecstasy

Buffets and all-you-can-eats

Babies who needs them we got ways of drownin' them before they even make the shore

Kill your legacies

"You got to do you"* mantras

Run get yours leave your children behind for someone else to rearview mirrors don't use buy new and exchange few

Keep runnin' the wheel don't ever get off to see it's attached to the side of wall going nowhere just nowhere at all

Stop clapping

Somebody's slappin' smackin' hands hit me full force switches broke off from a tree

It's grandma

Yes ma'am...

Grandma, I promise not to let the good life lull me to sleep and allow me to fail to recall all you labored for was to see me be free

My sophisticated sofa won't put me to ease

My briefcase

My fake eyelashes with Mac-brushed lips

The cars in my driveway are not just there to please

I will take the treasure you placed in my hands

The seeds of your sufferings

And throw them past what I can see

From the sea to shining sea shining*

I won't overlook
Your cliffs
I won't be satisfied

With keeping up with who's by my side
Farther
Deeper
Higher
Pressin' pushin' stirrin' strainin' further past my present-day liberties
The real choices I will create I naught just keep rollin' in all I can take and make
Stop, let me think
I have a costly inheritance far more expensive than jewels or gold
You can't buy it or bargain or steal
It's not sold in any store
It's been planted deep in my soul
The memories of a people
Bedded in unmarked graves
Their songs their stories have a sequel
I stand on mountains
I leap over valleys
I wade in waters
I dive into deep rivers
I cascade the waterfalls
"Didn't my Lord deliver Daniel?"*
Grandma, my head, my head!
Their testimony is it not for today
Shall I take what's been given and kneel at the beach of this forlorn land
And say it is enough, I'm satisfied
With Bling like everyone else and get what everyone else is gettin
Is that it, is that all there is?

404 years of steppin' and the road ends here
With me satisfied with a Posturepedic Sleep Number bed 79
No, wake up!
"Awake, O sleeper,
and arise from the dead,
and Christ will shine on you."*
At the end of the day, evening does not come, this is no time to sleep
We have been destined for the dawn, a new horizon is breaking
The sun and moon stand still, time opens its hands to eternity
From the storage closet, comes a bottle of tears
Outpouring
The skies burst
The earth floods again
Heaven and earth kiss
We have done more than our share
Our labor has not been in vain
We have reached down to the depths
And brought up our hands
In humble sacrifice before Almighty God
Smoking coals and ashes
The soul of a people and their offspring shivering naked on ocean beaches
Who stand before God?
And say,
For what reason have you brought us to this place, for such a time as this?
Rain on us
"The floods have lifted up, O LORD, The floods have lifted up their voice the floods lift up their pounding waves."*
Let our season for blooming on the earth begin.

*See endnotes.

Awake! O Sleeper

Oh Abraham would raise his hands
And mourn this very day
For his children left the promised land
In search of their own way
They kick and scream like wayward sons
Always wanting to sleep

And dream away these evil days
In hopes that God can't see
There are chains upon your children, Lord
Chains upon your children
There are chains upon your children
We're in chains

Do you hear the lion roar?

Awake O Sleeper
Stand with me we'll fight the war
Awake O Sleeper
Your suffering will come again
And never fall away
For we trade our many comforts
Like the one who bled for grace

There will come a day my God will come
And put me in my place
My God I pray, You'll call my name
Instead of turn away
Let no man bring me harm
I bear the marks of Jesus
Let no man bring me harm
I bear the marks of the Lord

Arise O' Sleeper
There are chains upon your children, Lord
Chains upon your children*

*See endnotes.

In the Belly

§

"THEN JONAH PRAYED TO THE Lord his God from inside the fish: 'In my great trouble I cried to the Lord and he answered me; from the depths of death I called, and Lord, you heard me! You threw me into the ocean depths; I sank down into the floods of waters and was covered by your wild and stormy waves. Then I said, "O Lord, you have rejected me and cast me away. How shall I ever again see your holy Temple?"

"'I sank beneath the waves, and death was very near. The waters closed above me; the seaweed wrapped itself around my head. I went down to the bottoms of the mountains that rise from the ocean floor. I was locked out of life and imprisoned in the land of death. But, O Lord my God, you have snatched me from the yawning jaws of death! When I had lost all hope, I turned my thoughts once more to the Lord. And my earnest prayer went to you in your holy Temple. (Those who worship false gods have turned their backs on all the mercies waiting for them from the Lord!) I will never worship anyone but you! For how can I thank you enough for all you have done? I will surely fulfill my promises. For my deliverance comes from the Lord alone.' And the Lord ordered the fish to spit up Jonah on the beach, and it did."*

*See endnotes.

Locked Out

§

Locked out of life and imprisoned in the land of death my number is

Quick run get down don't shoot hands up face down like an inner need in pardon my number is 10923

Locked in a cell for something I didn't do shut up and listen to my song to my rap and my tune

No one ever did right by me not mama nor papa not as white or black man do right by me all my life long

So where was I the night they found a needle in my arm?

I was lickin' up the syrup of a plate that's always been empty, empty sweetness is the worst high of them

All

Cut up bruised blackened and tattooed who wants me who calls my name into the night who claims me

You, you wanna take me home to a pew in your church no I tell you there is one million of us marchin'

No! One million of us locked up behind cells and bars with no one comin' no one carin' no one even

noticing we're missing

absent voices mute in these multiplyin' cages they buildin' for profit

Hey, hey, you out there don't you know I'm GONE!

Yeah didn't think so...just go on?

I Remember

Behind two barbed-wire fences and pistol-armed lookouts at
east and west
You sit
Cemented iron bars
Locked in
But not locked out
We remember the day you fell off the family wire midair

Night Falls
Night falls
Into a new day

Motherless

Sometimes I feel like a motherless chil'
A long way from home
A long way from home
Sometimes I feel like I almos' gone
Sometimes I feel like I almos' gone
Sometimes I feel like I almos' gone
A long way from home.*

*See endnotes.

Chains

§

There are chains upon your children Lord *
Chains upon your children
There are chains upon your children
We're in chains.
But we don't even know it
Take me to the river*
Talk to the river
Take me to the river to be baptized
None but the righteous
None but the righteous
Shall see God
May the seas cause our chains to float
That we may see our present-day slavery
Take me to the river
Take me to the river
To be baptized.

*See endnotes.

Delilah

§

The bright orange sun is passed its path
Late for the sunset
Smiling at the moon waiting to shine
A feather falls between the limbs of a leafless tree
The figure of a woman shaded in shadow
Tanned deep from the full sun
Her skin glistening facing a gated paradise
"You leavin', I told you they are going to give us the keys, just stay
four more years"
Her beauty far from gone lies just beneath the skim milk choco-
late skin surface
"They'll give us free lunches I tell you, as she points to hundreds
of empty recyclable milk cartons"
The high cheekbones between the broad road nose settles in a
round full lips drink from a cup nearly empty every day
"Free methadone"
"Come on believe me it's not a merry round, we are going some-
where this time"
Been quite a number years since her cup overflowed with prom-
ises and agendas
Her raggedy dress once sparkled under spotlights as she stood
on their platforms
And testified to their credit

She believed their sentimental saccharine speeches
Of compassion and entitlements
The Party left her and hers high and dry
They topped her off and took the Party elsewhere
Oh my funny valentine there's no chocolates in this box
Or money left on the stand
Brokenhearted don't be
They'll be back pledging with wooing caches of butterfly ballots
This time and the next but
Where, oh where have all your lovers gone and left you
Homeless
Orphaned
Imprisoned
Impoverished
Addicted
Stumbling in darkness
A drunken stupor
Take what's left of you
Pour out the wine
Stand before the choir
And sing again this time
"Say my funny valentine, are you smart?"*
You pledged your heart your soul and your voted voices
Look, they have left you hung you out on a leafless branch
"Do I get to keep the yard sign?"
Waitin' to be blown like the wind.

*See endnotes.

The Black Man

§

WHY I BELIEVE THE BLACK man is the key to America's revival? In the sense that as the door opens he will lead others to liberty, he is the turnkey. This is not to the exclusion of the black woman.

We understand from the Genesis account that the woman was housed in the man. She is created from him and therefore by nature is included. Important in viewing the attack and subsequent strategic war on the black man we see him in the context of American history. Uprooted, his wife raped and stolen. We see his seed scattered all over and his manhood stripped. Today it is the black family that suffers from the father's absence. Malachi reminds us of this curse between fathers and their children.

"His preaching [speaking of Elijah] will turn the hearts of fathers to their children, and the hearts of children to their fathers. Otherwise I will come and strike the land with a curse." We pray and desire for this returning of the black man to his rightful place of honor in the home and society.

He is the victim. Out of him come the branches of other offended parties.

Who was lynched?

The black man.

Who was castrated?

The black man.

Who was forcibly and intentionally removed from his family?

The black man

To remove identity, security, stability for his seed for multiple generations

It is the black man, I say,

Who still suffers today?

There is wrapped in the black man's history a link to the greatest story ever told. As we read the pages of Scripture we see God choosing a man. This man was to be his chosen vessel to birth a nation, Father Abraham. From Father Abraham a child of promise secured by faith was born, Isaac. Isaac was to be the great father of the twelve tribes of Israel.

His name is changed and he produces twelve sons. Joseph is hated by his brothers and sold into slavery.

He is unfairly accused and is subjected to *slavery* and later imprisonment. However, God is with him.

He is given a gift by God to interpret dreams. His gift brings him to Pharaoh's court where he is enthroned as second in command over all Egypt. What man even his own brothers intended for his destruction God sovereignly allows for the blessing of his nation. Joseph's position opens the avenues for his father and their nation to come to Egypt for preservation. This preservation within two generations is challenged and the people of God find themselves greater and stronger than their neighbors. Two nations within one land. Thus the Egyptians deal a cruel hand to the Israelites by enslaving them. For four hundred years they cry out for deliverance. At the appointed time, God sends a humble man, Moses, to bring Egypt and its gods to their knees. With great triumph and victory, he leads this nation on their Exodus. Over their history God deals with his people using slavery. For their disobedience and idol worship, He sends them back to slavery. For their repentance and contrition and changed ways, He leads them to freedom. These themes of slavery and freedom are throughout Scripture.

The book of Ruth reveals a God who is a kinsman: *redeemer*. A close relative who will take up the widow and her cause and fill the obligations of her dead husband. He covers her and provides a resting place. He redeems her land.

The book of Esther offers an example of God's provision *for justice and judicial legislation*. A young virgin is brought to the king as a result of an unyielding queen. She is positioned to bring deliverance to her nation. Even in their sojourning in foreign land, God's watchful eyes look toward their future. She is a change agent as she forms legislation to protect them from extermination.

Ezra and Nehemiah give us accounts for *restoration*. Kings favorably disposed toward these men and their burdens empty vaults of storehouses to restore what has been destroyed and stolen. Although the disobedience of this nation brought such trouble upon themselves, God is seemingly on their side as he opens up the windows of heaven to preserve them and ensure their survival.

God's people were a sojourning, temporary people. Longing for their homeland. They were strangers in a foreign land. They were in expectation of a deliverer and Messiah.

As the story continues Jesus enters as a figure with questionable upbringing. A mother pregnant before marriage during her espousal period. A father who vanishes further into the story. His birth is in a stable with animals. He is an outcast. He loves the unlovable and does extraordinary things in people's lives. Despised and rejected by his own, he was marred and disfigured. They whipped him. They beat him.

He was unjustly murdered and made to carry a load he did not deserve. Yet he suffered and looked for something greater than his own future. He looked into the past on the cross and saw all of man's sin.

He picked up the curse for all mankind and laid it on His shoulder because this was pleasing to His Father. He saw you and he saw me.

For the questions of today, he saw and sees the black man.

From the beginning until the end God's story is intertwined with ours. We are not replacing Israel, but we can be convinced to say that like the people of Israel we were enslaved. Like his nation we were delivered. We have been redeemed. God has brought us to a Promised Land. He has given us many Josephs to provide for our preservation. He has sent the Moseses to deliver us from bondage declaring emancipation. He has raised up Esthers to rally for our justice and judicial legislation.

Prophetic African American voices stir in us visions and dreams of faith of a world laid unseen. We have seen our struggle strengthen the victims still in segregation and oppression. We have left our tools behind in the valleys to help them rally for freedom.

Let freedom rise!

Jesus, like the black man, was born with animals. In stables. Jesus had stigmas surrounding his family. His father is not present. His single mother did suffer from public opinion. He was redlined and ostracized by the religious. He was wrongly accused and forcibly removed from his rightful place in the synagogue.

He has borne the nails that we have.

The wood of our ships were laid on His back. Our blood and water coursed freely from his side.

The sting and slashing of stripes punishing innocence he understands.

The painful searing and separation of mothers and children, husbands and wives.

He cried. He knows. As we look upon his mangled body strung up on a cross we feel him pulling us closer not casting away. Acceptance not rejection. With every tear comes a calling to the black man, to feel and know a Savior that is acquainted with all his griefs.

To be cast out and denied there is no doubt, Jesus holds the greatest account and witness against this world. Yet He holds something even more. On the cross there is an eternal revelation that spans all of eternity. With the holes of that eternity puncturing his human flesh he releases the very power that raised him from the grave. He speaks.

"Father forgive them for they know not what they do."

They are not able to conceive what it is they are doing. Crucifying God.

He releases the greatest miracle. The tidal wave is larger than even Noah's floods, pouring from his side. The water and its gushing is enough to cover the whole world and wash its sin away.

To whom is this power given?

To the Son because he suffered. He died and rose again.

So, tell me, who has a great wound?

Who identifies with Jesus?

Who can identify?

I tell you it is the black man.

I could say we are not forgotten.

But I would rather God has not forgotten us as a people.

He remembers.

The largest group of humans in all the annals of time violently abducted (by some accounts by their own brothers) and sold into the most brutal slave trade, the descendants of these now bearing lineage of two continents, Africa and the Americas.

To these afflicted and broken ones God is saying, I remember. I am an all-seeing God. I know all things. He speaks tenderly and extends an open invitation.

As we look at our history and reflect upon such parallels in God's dealing with his own people, let us take heart. He has preserved us as a people. There is upon His face a smile as we walk into the days ahead. A new horizon is upon us. God is up to something in this nation. His purposes that span hundreds of years are coming into full view. Perspectives, his vantage point, His agenda for the black man is just a page away. A new story is being written. Yesterday's themes are but backtracks of the melodies coming from heaven.

Will you believe, could you dare to imagine that the course of all our suffering could navigate paths in the waters of salvation for the whole world to see?

Sweet Little Jesus Boy

Sweet little Jesus Boy
They made You be born in a manguh
Sweet little Holy chil'
Didn't know who You wus
Didn't know You'd come to save us Lawd
To take our sins away

Our eyes wus bline
We couldn't see
We didn't know who You wus
Long time ago You wus bawn
Bawn in a manguh low

Sweet little Jesus Boy
De worl' [the world] treat You mean, Lawd
Treat me mean too
But please, Suh, fuhgive us Lawd
We didn't know 'twas You

Sweet little Jesus Boy
Bawn [born] long time ago
Sweet little Holy chil'
An' we didn't know who You wus.

Tell Me Who but Jesus?

§

WHO SHALL BELIEVE OUR REPORT? And upon whom shall the arm of the LORD be manifested? With all this he shall grow up before him as a tender sprout and as a root out of a dry ground. There is no outward appearance in him, nor beauty. We shall see him, yet nothing attractive about him that we should desire him. He is despised and rejected among men, a man of sorrows, and acquainted with weakness, and we hid as it were our faces from him; he was despised, and we esteemed him not.

Surely he has borne our sicknesses and suffered our pain: and we considered him stricken, smitten of God, and cast down. But he was wounded for our rebellions; he was bruised for our iniquities; the chastisement of our peace was upon him; and by his stripes healing was provided for us. All we like sheep have become lost; we have turned each one to his own way, and the LORD transposed in him the iniquity of us all. He was oppressed, and he was afflicted, yet he did not open his mouth; he was brought as a lamb to the slaughter, and as a sheep before her shearers is dumb, so he did not open his mouth. He was taken from prison and from judgment, and who shall count his generation? For he was cut off out of the land of the living; for the rebellion of my people he was smitten. And he made his grave with the wicked, and his death with the rich; even though he had never done evil, neither was any deceit in his mouth.

With all this the LORD chose to bruise him; subjecting him to grief. When he shall have offered his soul for atonement, he shall sow his seed, he shall prolong his days, and the will of the LORD shall be prospered in his hand. He shall see of the travail of his soul and shall be satisfied. And by his knowledge shall my righteous slave justify many, for he shall bear their iniquities. Therefore I will divide him a portion with the great, and he shall divide the spoil unto the strong because he has poured out his soul unto death, and he was numbered with the rebellious, having borne the sin of many, and made intercession for the transgressors."*

*See endnotes.

I Believe He's like Me

§

THE IDENTIFICATION OF THE BLACK experience in its relationship to God's story and the story of his people bring cohesion and harmony to our souls. As if we know now what we didn't know that we knew before.

We are wanted. We have not been just thrown into the air and randomly scattered. There are higher calls and causes for our suffering. The black man's *solvation* is found in Jesus. Jesus alone understands and sympathizes with our **miseries.**

The Misery of Being Black

§

I woke up one morning. No cause of my own. My eyes opened and I let out a groan.

All the trees were green. The grass was mowed.

I stepped out of my house and into the road. Didn't look at myself

To see what was wrong that I couldn't see.

But all around there were two sides of me.

I felt like the man standing in line.

Couldn't understand why he was first in line.

I went to the store didn't intend to buy

Strange how they watch me and follow behind

Went to eat at a friend's had to travel a little

Didn't notice till I left the signs for hoaxes and the circus

Employment job ads for me were all lined up

With sliding fees

Never be at the top never make any decisions

Even church was just come sit and listen

So I decided to take a look in the mirror and see what was wrong with me

I breathed I sneezed had no deformity

Not wheelin' in a chair not blind or disabled

What had I done why all these decrees

About being fair and legislating justice

Were these really necessities?

Seemed to be based on perception 'cause all I could see was a man born just like everyone else
The fault could not lie with me
So the world stands with its finger in the air pointing to a God they say doesn't care
Pointing at Him and then pointing at me
God didn't know better
When his paint hit the canvas and colored me
Colored me wrong for their world to belong
Colored me into the shape and not free to imagine
Colored me colored me colored me wrong
God must have known we told him we gave him our instructions
We don't like darkies, coloreds, or browns
God didn't notice didn't care to oblige their arrogant orders and worldly prides
He colors what He pleases and as He desires to see
He colored the cardinals the lilies the bees the butterflies the roses even the fish at the bottom of the sea
Like a master artist longing to see beautiful colors like flowers in the spring
I laid down that night started to cry then stopped
I'm not the wrong color
I am the man I'm supposed to be
For I reflect not man's simple thoughts
But God's creativity.
Hallelujah I'm black.
I've got a story to tell
When God dipped his brush he had to several times for my color to see
Tinted with hues shadows and brights
I am a living breathing testimony
Of a god not blinded but sees
And when I rise in the morning I sing
I sing thank yous to the God

Who made me
The color that I am that I may reflect to the world
His colorful mind
His reality.

Oh sing with me children sing with me now
God is a good God. God is a good, good God.
When I get to imagine I'll be even darker and comely
For from the centuries to eternity
I'll look in His eyes and see His beauty reflected
In the way He made me.
Hallelujah I'm black wouldn't want to be any other
Color or colored complexion to be seen
God made me with the mean world in view and
Decided to stroke me in a color He knew
Would challenge many and provoke not just a few
He knew I would be hated and despised for my skin
And that is why He gave me a song deep within
A song to sing in the mornin'
A song to sing when I'm affright
A song to sing when I'm dyin' and
Sick in the night
Don't matter how they hate
No matter if the hate still hurts
He wanted me to be like His Son
To feel his pain at its worsts
Despised and rejected by a world he owns
Cursed and cast out by names no one yet knows
He made me to understand and stand at the Cross
Not judging
Not asking
Not pondering this great, great loss

He made me dark so I could feel
a small, small fragment of His cost
His suffering
Relating by feeling I now can know
And recognize Him
His face, his hands, his piercings as the blood flows
I know
Beyond any knowledge or information found in a book
I sense Him I hear His voice
For He is familiar to me.
He has come to me thousands of times
Standing beside me in all my journey of sufferings
Whispering crying solacing
Standing
He knows who I am
A black man created by His hands to be
A man standing close by His side, as a familiar friend, a dark-skinned
companion on his way to the Cross
Treated with scorn and shame, judged like Him for something
God chose Him to be.

The Door

§

There is a door. On one side it confines. However, on the other side it opens.

"Jesus said, 'I am the door. I am the Way to the Father. I hold the keys to death, hell and the grave.'*"

He stands on both sides. He confined himself in time to provide opening to eternity.

Through him we are able to enter a life beyond imagination.

This door hinges on His suffering. His suffering swings on eternal realities. Holy archways.

It is not of this world. His ways are in opposition to the kingdom of this world.

His kingdom exchanges not money but mercy.

Not position or power but servanthood.

Not self-fulfillment but self-denial.

On this threshold if suffering is the hinge then forgiveness is the space itself.

The space that we walk through.

The empty place where man meets God.

It has been prepared and Jesus himself burst this entranceway.

Without relation to time and space it defies all laws and matter. Gravity cannot bring it down.

Death loses. Cemeteries open. Forgiveness is an eternal matter. Leaving the soul of man it connects and leads us to heavenly places.

In the economy of God, we find the upside kingdom. He who sins the most, loves the most.

He who holds the greatest offense has the greatest seed for life.

Jesus on the cross. Didn't do nothing. They scourged. Whipped, nailed him.

He was marred beyond disfiguration. As we see Jesus hanging, his body dangling from this tree, we see the dark clouds curling in, covering the expanse between heaven and earth.

There we carry the deep wound of our people. To the Cross. To the Cross.

A scene unfolds.

The graves opening, the memories, the wretched wreaking history and we hear the words of destiny

Over the African American and his painful story.

Black man, forgive them.

I can't, Lord. You are right. We can't. So we stand looking at Jesus. And hear him say what we cannot in and of ourselves.

Jesus says, "Father forgive them for they know not what they do."*

And it is there in His prayer that I make peace and say, Lord, it's in your hands. Jesus prayed it. As a black man. I stand before Jesus. I enter into the prayer of an innocent man. I let his prayer cover me. I release my soul to him, and say what you did on that Cross for all mankind for every sin is enough. It spans for eternity. Jesus explodes his grace over all generations. His sacrifice is sufficient. He asks us not to forget but only to release our wounds and sorrows to Him.

It is there Jesus entered the holy place in heaven. Wrongs and injustices for all time for all people are set right in a heavenly courtroom. He himself has opened the throne by shedding His blood. We stand in this holy place before a holy God. Heaven has heard our case. There is One who sits in judgment over the whole earth.

He who is our peace beholds our griefs and promises in His time to make all things beautiful.

We hold a great piercing. In that piercing is the power to release the seeds of forgiveness to the land,

To this nation. WE as the victims have received the grace, the grace to then release a healing or withhold it. WE have suffered greatly. The Lord has entrusted us much on this side of heaven to release for His glory.

Black man, release the glory of God!

*See endnotes.

Dear Jesus,

I tremble before you, writhing in the pain of all that has been laid upon my back. For over four hundred years you have heard every pitiful cry, your eyes have witnessed in all places all things done to my people,

Your hands alone hold all my children drowned in the waters. Come now, Lord Jesus, take me to the waters of your pierced side. Wash me, cleanse me, and remove these dead man grave clothes. Let your blood plead over my life and my people, victory by the word of our testimony. What Satan has designed to annihilate, God has provided a man in heaven's court, Jesus, for such a time as this. By his word, I take my stand as a black man and release the grace of God over this land of America for healing and restoration. I see fathers rising up taking their stand. I see a great river of God, a river teeming with life opening. As it is spreading to every part of this nation whoever gets in this river is baptized and made fresh and new.

From the hidden graves, out of the ground comes a great up-swelling of justice flowing and declaring, Your King has come! Glory Hallelujah! He has risen indeed! Jesus riding on a white horse declaring to the nations. I am Alpha and Omega. Let heaven and earth agree the blood of Jesus is greater and flows freely for all. Nothing is impossible with God! God reigns, He is Lord and in His presence, all my tears, all my sorrows they are washed away!

I release by my words and decree, Give me now what you have decreed from before the worlds began! The destiny of the black man! All the enemy has stolen restore! My eyes, my heart, my soul, my life, my joy! Give me what belongs to me what you have kept in store.

Lord Jesus, we ask you to release through this word, every eternal blessing and inheritance that you have for this people African Americans. Father we ask that the heavenly storehouses be opened now and the grain would flow. Your grace would be upon this people to possess every place of influence, every gift and talent, every field and produce. Bless us in the city and the field. Pour out what you have reserved for this day and now. To the praise and glory of your wonderful name. May we reap the harvest of our laboring forefathers. Give to us our inheritance.

To Him who sits on the throne be all praise, JESUS.

I ask you to break every generational curse in my family line. Only You alone know my family history and all the sins of my forefathers. I ask you to remove from me the guilt, shame, and condemnation placed upon my life from my forefathers. I ask you to free me from all fears and torments associated with the wicked deeds of past actions done by others upon the members of my family line. I confess that the blood of Jesus covers all the sin done to my family and all the sin committed by my forefathers.

I acknowledge the great injustices and sufferings of my personal history in this nation. I release this debt owed to me in wages and inheritance. I release this offense to you. I receive the grace of God for all the wrong I have suffered and the wrongs done to my family. I enter into the prayer that Jesus prayed and ask you to cover my life by the blood of the Lamb and his sacrifice; all that I am, all that I have come from, all that I am destined to be I place in your hands. Restore unto me the joy of your salvation. Let my children be the beginning of a new day, walking in the destiny of God. The dream of your heart.

In Jesus's name I pray.

Diamonds

§

SHE WORE GRIEF AROUND HER like a blanket. Wrapped from shoulder to shoulder it held firmly in place. Tears rolled unconsciously down her cheeks, as searing pain jolted through her side. "Stop wasting time, you scum!" Her master belted from his full belly. It seemed to flow over his belt more and more as he spoke. His raspy voice mixed with her aching side brought all her faculties to immediate attention as she dipped her brush once more into the hot, soapy water and onto the wooden floor. Alas, this was her destiny.

Three-hundred-sixty-four days a year she was to scrub the floor. It made no difference. In fact, she could see no marked improvement from before to after. Her days were spent looking at cracks of dirt; she knew every inch, every groove of the planks. Therefore, no measure of pain would erase the memory of where and what she saw that day.

For just before the boot caught her thin ribs, a glint of sparkle caught her eye. Because she knew the floor so well, she knew just where to look when her day began tomorrow as it did the day before.

Rising as she finished, she was different. She rose in anticipation. She stood in hope. Same floor. Same merciless master. But she was different. A strange sensation came over her mouth but she dare not let it escape. A smile. She lowered her head. Drooped her shoulders and left. Wanting to skip, she lumbered across the yard. Almost dark out, she had ended early and decided to gather some berries for her dinner. Mama would be pleased with the berries and grateful to see her. She was the joy of her mother's eyes.

All the stripes of a whip could not take away the joy. For when her mother saw her, the biggest smile came across her face and a solitary tear would fall. It was as if all day long her mother thought of only one thing. Her baby girl. The berries were all ripe and full; she stuffed her mouth until thick purple juice ran from her lips and stained her hands. Still, there were just enough for mama to put in a pot. If only there were some of the white grains she sometimes saw on the floor. She did not know what it was but when she saw it she rubbed her hands clean and then dipped her fingers in her mouth to get them wet enough for the white grit to stay on her hands. Then when no one was looking she would lick and lick them. *One day I will get mama some.* She stopped almost in shock. Never before had she ever thought of a *one day*. Never had she imagined any day to be different than her past. *One day.*

Something had happened to her. Startled, she ran toward their small quarters. Mama turned at the door just in time to see her and extend her big brown arms.

Up before dawn, she sat waiting for her chore. She sat expectantly. Then not to give any hint she arrived a little late, received her usual scolding and smack across the face. With tears of joy and pain streaming down their lanes on her face she started the scrubbing not one brushstroke slower or faster. Her steady pace as ever before. As she had imagined it all night long, as she had planned without any breath of alarm, she dipped her brush with just enough extra water to make the sparkled speck float. Quickly she grabbed the brush pretending to rush it to the water. Her tiny fingers fastened around the piece just as she began the descent again. Her fingers slipped into her apron. She tried her best to be slow and lethargic but surges of energy kept filling her little arms with strength. As she rose that day, her eyes lowered to the floor. It looked different. It was shining.

Her fingers were sore from her first days of discovery. She pinched so tightly that the gems pierced through her fingertips. She did not care. Every day now she got up earlier and earlier. Watching and waiting. Waiting and watching for the day to begin. Her task, scrubbing the floor, had been transformed into discovering diamonds.

Three-hundred-sixty-four days later. Her pouch was bursting. She did not know what they were. She just kept gathering. Too scared to upset Mama. She thought through a plan to see them in the light. Papa would come home from another farm for Christmas day. On that day she would go a little farther in the woods in the day and see them. She was nervous. Mama noticed but, too busy preparing for Papa, gave little attention. All year she had been waiting to see him. The day grew on and the sun rose in the sky. Still no Papa.

Not wanting to waste the one day she could be in the sun. The little girl begged mama to let her gather some berries.

"All right, if you must," Mama said. "But remember, Papa comes home tonight. He's wanting to see his little girl."

"Mama I'm not little anymore," the little girl smiled.

"Wells you'll always be my little girl, now go on, chil', you see I'm busy?"

Busy she was fussing over one pot that had next to nothing in it. Massa hadn't even given one piece of meat. Said the farm didn't do better this year. We was to have their leftovers the next day. All good. 'cept Papa would be gone by then.

Out in the open, the sun gleamed through the trees. She was wrapped in a thin coat; the cold had not mattered. She was free. Free to dream. Free to imagine. At last free to see what she had gathered. Looking twice over her shoulders, she kneeled down in the snow. Unraveling the pouch on dead leaves her eyes were locked in a stare. Sparkling clear little rocks with points and smooth edges. She did not know what to call them. Suddenly she heard footsteps. Then a voice.

"What you doin' out here?"

She didn't have enough time to wrap them so she flung her fingers around the pouch and took off in a run, dropping some to the ground. Where was she going? Why had she been so foolish? Fear gripped her heart; she could hardly breathe. The nameless sounds of the footsteps followed her in pursuit, but the voice she knew. The voice had a name. It was her master. She fell. Her knees were bleeding but she continued to crawl. She managed to scramble under some brush. She would get a beating for running away. Maybe Mama, too. But she would not tell. Never. She promised. A cold wind began to blow. The sun was going away. She would freeze to death if she stayed. Up ahead she could see a figure in the distance. In a dizzy haze, she saw a man cutting trees. Then another come and try to pull him away. She thought she heard a tree fall.

Uprooted. The first man started running. He was coming her way. It was her papa. Crying out from the brush she could hardly speak. Papa! Papa! His big black hands reached out and grabbed her body like a sack. She sank her tiny hands into his and let go of her pouch.

She woke up, not sure how long she had been asleep. Mama was different. The joy gone from her eyes. She hardly spoke. Just gave her her apron when she was strong enough and pointed to the kitchen door. She went back to the floor. No more. She was given a different task. She had to stand in the cold, rain, and snow and serve the others who were cast to the floor. Time, day after day, she had not a thought. Couldn't quite remember anything. Cared less if she ever remembered a day not like yesterday. Not having a mirror, she hadn't noticed she had grown. Standing, shoulders drooping, eyes lowered, she stood like a stone.

News came that the farm had been lost. Master and his own would be moving on and a new master would arrive. Mama perked up, hoping her little girl would get a new task. The floors were cleaned; the house arrayed. The slaves stood displayed. Coming down from their carriage, a man and his wife, three little children, and a few of their slaves. The rest were coming. Eyes lowered, shoulders drooping, shawls of grief had holes that day. For just as the others pulled away, the little girl thought she saw a man she once knew. Laying down his reins he jumped off the carriage and took off his hat. He raised his eyes, and squared his shoulders, held out his arms and yelled, "For us slavery is over! That little pouch you gave me bought this whole place and now come here, my darling, and mama too; let me show you just where you will set your shoes! These people are good folks from up north. They are here to help us to get more folks just like us who keep their eyes on the floor and their mouths closed to stand up straight and look high into the sky. Theys gonna stay here with us and work to show others the way!"

    With her mouth wide open, the not-so-little girl fell to the floor.

    The others looked on in disbelief. And mama had a look of displeasure.

    "Why you gone did all that; I just asked you to get me some wood!"

    With that, Papa let out a roar of laughter and tried to pick up Mama.

    She was crying and fussing and laughin' all the way up the steps.

Living in a World That Is beyond Our Imagination

§

IF THE PAST FOUR HUNDRED years are Chapter One of black history then we must get ready for Chapter 2. Have we not been given diamonds, treasures found on our journey?

The saga of the African American journey from shore to shore is replete with horrors. As we turn the pages through time we see a fracturing of a people not only physically but psychologically as well. Written in our DNA the information of our travels and voyages, our tears and heartbreaks are stored.

Today it seems the fires of our souls rage as we watch the self-destruction in our neighborhoods, the drug lords overtaking our lands. The black prison population is staggering, black-on-black crime, black abortion rates and poverty give evidence to an all-out attack and assault to exterminate a people. A riveting genocide is happening before our eyes.

From within and without a raging fire burns.
Yet there are flames hotter and brighter that enlighten a turn.
The black man is not to be fuel for destruction. He carries in his hands the pouch, a gem of a stone.
Mined in the dark caverns of the earth, his story forged brazen and beautiful, dazzling dares to defy logic and man's eyes of evaluation and estimation.

The consummation of his labors he still holds.

Like the little girl we let go of our pouch into the Father's hands.

Lord, we may vaguely remember the time and the scenes of our surrender.

For some it may not yet have occurred. But at this very moment, we release the treasures found in suffering into your hands.

We wait, rest assured for your return.

Redemption Riding on Horseback

As I looked into his eyes.
I saw all
Bruising beating
Death decay
Stranded
Struggling flinching flayed
Running limping crawling
Writhing screaming
Silence
Weeping stripping slipping
Raping not bathing boiling
Experimenting hanging oozing
Cringing crying dead
Wailing wondering doubting
Marching fleeing sitting
Beating 'busing
Falling singing
Overcoming
Shooting dancing sewing
Cooking failing selling
Sinning leaving
Speaking turning blowing
Swearing

Swaying
Stepping opening
Holding releasing
Expecting Him to see
All of us all there ever was or will ever be
In this moment
And for Him to breathe
On us smiling
"For surely he has borne our griefs and carried our sorrows."*

*See endnotes.

Go down Moses, Way down in Egypt Land

§

Tell old Pharaoh to let my people
When Israel was in Egypts land
Let my people go
Oppressed so hard they could not stand
Let my people go
Go down Moses
Way down in Egypt land
Tell old Pharaoh
"Let my people go"
"Thus spoke the Lord" bold Moses said
Let my people go
"If not I'll smite your first-born dead
Let my people go
No more in bondage shall they toil
Let my people go
Let them come out with Egypt's spoil"
Let my people go.*"

*See endnotes.

From Sea to See

§

Her breathing was fast, much too fast
Lean fingers clutched the sheets until her knuckles grew white, her teeth
clenched she gasps as if her head was drowning in waters
Slow deeper breathe
before she could catch another breath
She screamed out
Logs burned in the fire. A thin misty rain fell outside the cabin.
Pattering the tin roof the sounds could not soften the wrenching agony
Her bent legs shaking uncontrollably her face covered in sweat her breasts
exposed
Her body every inch was immersed in this one thing
This one task…
Another yell into the darkness of the night…
Silence
No babies cry
No tears of joy…
"As the pregnant woman approaches the time to give birth, she writhes
and cries out in her labor pains, thus were we before You, O LORD. We
were pregnant, we writhed in labor, and we gave birth, as it seems, only
to wind. We could not accomplish deliverance for the earth, nor were
inhabitants of the world born. Your dead will live; their corpses will rise.
You who lie in the dust, awake and shout for joy, for your dew is as the
dew of the dawn, And the earth will give birth to the departed spirits…"*

We, too, writhe in agony, but nothing comes of our suffering. We have not given salvation to the earth, nor brought life into the world.

But nothing comes from our suffering. We have not given salvation to the earth, nor brought life into the world. The question remains will anything be born from our suffering? Will we bring salvation to the earth and life to the world?

O death, where *is* thy sting? O grave, where *is* thy victory?*

Christ is risen from the dead!

Come awake! Come awake, my brothers and sisters,

Christ is risen from the dead

Trampling over death by death

Come awake, come awake!

Come and rise up from the grave!*

*See endnotes.

Frostbitten

§

Frostbitten the child is born
The winter has past, spring has come
Let us bathe him with our tears and nurse wanting him close
Cooing and codling warming and soaking him in refreshing streams
From deeper pools resting wells in the earth
Blacker than coals and furnace he remains OUR son
The child of our suffering and blood spilling
Raised by hammer and anvil
We see him unashamed
Chainless
Running free
Naked
No swimming or striving
No searching or diving
Unflinchingly his gait is strong and steady
Reborn for such a time as this
He has left the island
This black man walks
Yes he walks upon the seas.

The Bark of a Tree

§

From the bark of a tree, can you see me?
I'm the empty cradle that was formed from a tree
To hold this people of destiny.

Lazarus has risen!

1. Soon ah wil be done wit de troubles of de world, p. 1. Negro spiritual; public domain.

2. "The eyes of the Lord run to and fro throughout the whole earth," I Chronicles 16:9, p. 2.

3. "Be ready to give an answer," I Peter 3:15, p. 2.

4. "You shall know the truth and the truth will set you free." John 8:32, p. 4.

5. "The Lamb of God who takes away the sin of the world," John 1:29, p. 8.

6. Summertime (inference), p. 10, an aria composed in 1934 by George Gershwin for his opera *Porgy and Bess*, lyrics by Dubose Heyward.

7. Redbox, current do-it-yourself vendor for movies in America, p. 11.

8. There is a balm in Gilead, p. 14, Negro spiritual, public domain.

9. "You shall go out with joy and be led forth with peace," p. 16, Isaiah 55:12.

10. "Woe am I for I am undone and dwell among a people of unclean lips," p. 17, Isaiah 6:5.

11. "His Eye Is on the Sparrow," p. 19, a gospel hymn, public domain, words by Civilia D. Martin.

12. Reference to Curse of Ham, Genesis 9:25, p. 29.

13. "What can make me White as Snow," p. 29, a gospel hymn referenced "Nothing but the Blood of Jesus."

14. "This land was made for you and me," p. 37, reference from "This Land Is Your Land," one of America's most famous folk songs, by Woody Guthrie.

15. Revelation 5:7-9, p. 39.

16. "Pharaoh's chariots and his army he has hurled into the sea. The best of Pharaoh's officers are drowned in the Red Sea. The deep waters have covered them; they sank to the depths like a stone," p. 42, Exodus 15:14 NIV.

17. "Lazarus, come forth," p. 43, John 11, NAS.

18. "But Lord he stinks," p. 42, John 11, NAS.

19. "Jesus weeps," p. 43, John 11, NAS.

20. "Lord if only…" p. 43, John 11, NAS.

21. "Roll away the stone," p. 43, John 11- NAS.

22. "I am the resurrection," p. 43, John 11- NAS.

23. "Lazarus, Come forth," p. 43, John 11- NAS.

24. Shall we gather at the river, p. 45, Methodist hymn, text Robert Lowry.

25. "As I went down to the river to pray, " considered a Christian folk song, Appalachian song, African American spiritual, with possible slave roots, p. 49.

26. "You got to do you," p. 65, common slang.

27. "From sea to shining sea," p. 65, lyric found in "America the Beautiful."

28. "Didn't My Lord Deliver Daniel," p. 66, Negro spiritual, public domain.

29. "Awake, O sleeper, and arise from the dead, and Christ will shine on you," p. 67, Ephesians 5:13-14.

30. "The floods have lifted up, O LORD, The floods have lifted up their voice the floods lift up their pounding waves," p. 67, Psalm 93.

31. Awake Sleeper, p. 69, Methodist hymn (Kirk/Wilkerson).

32. The Book of Jonah, Chapter 1, Common English Bible, p. 70.

33. "Sometimes I feel Like a Motherless Chile," p. 73, Negro spiritual, public domain.

34. There are chains upon your children, p. 74 (Kirk/Wilkerson).

35. Take Me to the River, Negro spiritual, public domain, p. 74.

36. "Say my funny valentine, are you smart?" p. 76, "My Funny Valentine" is a show tune from the 1937 Richard Rogers and Lorenz Hart musical *Babes in Arms*.

37. "Father forgive them for they know not what they do," p. 80, Luke 23:34.

38. "Sweet Little Jesus Boy," p. 82, Negro spiritual, public domain.

39. Who has believed our message? p. 83, Isaiah 53:1-12 (Jubilee Bible).

40. "Jesus said, 'I am the door,'" p. 90, John 10:9.

41. "I am the Way to the Father," p. 90, John 14:6.

42. "I hold the keys to death hell and the grave," p. 90, Rev.1:17-18.

43. "For surely he has borne our griefs and carried our sorrows," p. 103, Isaiah 53:4.

44. "Go down Moses," p. 104, Negro spiritual, public domain.

45. "Come awake, come awake," reference to p. 69.

46. "As the pregnant woman approaches the time to give birth, she writhes and cries out in her labor pains, thus were we before You, O LORD. We were pregnant, we writhed in labor, and we gave birth, as it seems, only to wind. We could not accomplish deliverance for the earth, nor were inhabitants of the world born. Your dead will live; their corpses will rise. You who lie in the dust, awake and shout for joy, for your dew is as the dew of the dawn, And the earth will give birth to the departed spirits," p. 105, Isaiah 26:17.

47. "O death, where *is* thy sting? O grave, where *is* thy victory?" p. 106, I Cor. 15:55.

48. "He was bruised," p. 123, Isaiah 53:5.

49. "Like a sheep before her shearers is dumb," p. 123, Isaiah 53:7.

50. "The wolves of Bashan," p. 123, Psalm 22:16.

51. "The Mighty one now dwells among us. He rides on the wings of the wind," p.126, reference to Deut. 33:26.

Epilogue

§

IN THE SUMMER OF 1992, I traveled with a team on a short-term missionary trip to Kenya. It was there while staying just outside of Nairobi that I had a life-changing conversation with a Kenyan woman. We sat in the warm sun for a lovely chat. She shared with me her family, her tribe, her tribal language. I explained to her my family and upbringing. She then turned to me with a perplexed look and asked, but what is your tribe? I looked back to her and said, I have no tribe, I am an African American.

As if in slow motion the words came out of her mouth: "Then you are nothing; you are as a leaf on a tree, blowing away."

I was devastated. This profound disconnectedness had haunted me all of my life. She spoke the unspoken secrets of my heart. I had no roots. Growing up in a predominantly white suburb I had assimilated into a culture where I was accepted yet did not quite belong.

Being measured in a society where success is the finish line and focal point, I was a success. Inwardly, however, there was a hollowness. The Kenyan woman touched my heart that day. It was as if someone had just planted me by a road, without intention. I was just one of millions disconnected from myself and not ever 100 percent who I should have been or where I belonged. Coming to faith in Jesus, I wish I could say made a difference. But unfortunately Jesus became like a room in my soul. If black history, my personal and historical, were the bedroom, Jesus was the living room. They are housed together but unconnected. What was the connection between Malcom X and my Jesus faith? For so long they were just stored together but never combined. How do I reconcile my history, the essence of who I am, with the gospel?

Sadly enough, watching TV preachers and circling the church scene did not speak to my paradoxical dilemma. As I began taking the gospel into the slave narrative, I realized God has a lot to say. His terms are related to my life.

Even the simple experience of changing my name—Bertha—gave me a revelation.

I don't remember how long it took the first day of school, but it wasn't long. The other children felt uncomfortable with my name. I went to school Bertha. I came home as Shelle. Renamed with a nickname to make the crowd. Naming.

Your name is your identity. The slaves were renamed. Stripped of all previous significances, in order that they would forget all they ever were.

I began to realize that the story of His people's experience is related to mine. The Savior's experience is related to mine.

His fingerprints are all over my life. It is not by accident or unfortunate events that I am African American. He planted me. I began to realize I am not lost or forgotten. The fruit I have as a descendant of slaves is for the healing of nations.

The disconnectedness and feeling of distantness from the American way of life is like watching a soccer game. Sure, one can argue that I could play. That I am free to choose to play, but still there is, at the end of the day, a nagging reminder that it's not my game. I can play. But I never get to choose the game.

Sure, things are better.
Yes, we as a people are making strides.
No, I am not angry.
The premise is this: I'm not playing soccer anymore. Neither am
I watching the game.

I don't want to be regulated by the rules that say you have to let me play. That's the law.

We as a people have been happy and satisfied with being allowed to play another man's game, without reckoning with our destiny as a people.

What we have not asked nor reconciled with is, why are we here? Why are we the red ink of injustice flowing through America's pages of bank deposits?

We are the black eye in the tale of the founding fathers.

We are the Tamar with both staff and ring saying,

I have proof of your misdeed.

We are the witnesses of a trial yet to come.

But for now I'm stating

There is a reason.

We have come this far as a people for such a time as this.

I believe it is our calling to release this nation to a destiny greater than we could have ever imagined.

Planted in this soil are our mothers and fathers

Just like Abel their blood cries out

Are we satisfied with justice when redemption is in view?

I believe the black man holds the key to this nation's true revival.

A Tribute: The Daughter's Tale

§

ONCE UPON A TIME IN a land far away, there were no full moons or sunsets, only skies dismal and gray.

But towering above a city below stood a formidable castle from which poured a glow; the light of the Presence of a Glorious King dwelt inside. His light filled the castle and all who live outside.

Down the small little streets with the homes and warm cabins, the light of the King made life simple and sweet.

But as sure as pages in a book do turn, the King was called to assist in a war.

Far from the meadow, the brook, and the shore, He would travel to find the battle roar.

His fight was not by bow or armor but simply to stand and provide light through the night. To strengthen the troops and the battle-weary and worn, His guiding light would grant victory by morn. He would return, rest assured, as He kissed His daughter and Son good-bye. Theirs now was the task to provide light at the dawn.

The Son left to provide escort to the King to the border, and the daughter rose early to stand in her corner. Far up high on the roof she could see from city to city to the mountains in glee.

She was so pleased to see all the light she was given that a day passed but seemed as only a minute.

But again as the pages of life do turn, she noticed a glint at the end of one turn.

A sparkle of light flashed from the street in response, and she thought, *Could it be that I might see the light I cast?* So from that moment on she determined at noon to look for the cart that carried her reflection in tow. She must see her own beauty and light bestowed.

Every evening when her task was fulfilled, she would disguise herself and cover her light and venture the streets into the night. She grew weary by day from her evening sprees, but her heart yearned to see her true unveiling. At last one evening as she searched far and wide, she almost turned back when a glint caught her eye. From a carriage no poorer, a rickety cart fell a small piece of something that shined when it fell. And she thought, *This is it, my soul, it is well.* She followed the cart not noticing how far until out into the open of a field. But at last she had traveled too far. Too late to turn back round to restore to the city so her fate lay ahead. And she thought, *I must see.*

So an exchange of promises was made with those who agreed for her to see what treasure lay beneath the coverings, she would unsheathe.

They removed old tattered blankets and with a gasp she could see the pieces of a once beautiful full mirror now lay fragmented and splintered. As she removed the veil from her head, her light blazed across the broken glass in a rage. Her desperation, her driving desire to see her own beauty was now a fire consuming and a bleeding vanity.

Her light was for others. Not a self-consummation. She would lose her sight and be handcuffed to a tree.

She was now employed by the bearers of shining things. To cast light and shadows for those who have need. Trapped and forgotten the tears no longer could be seen, for all her purpose was lost and even her destiny.

No light in the city did appear the next morn and the shopkeepers and schoolchildren and the bakers clambered about in the darkness.

The birds did not sing and the fields did not bloom and across the whole land fell a spell and gloom. If tears could form rivers then to the ocean they would flow the daughters eyes never stopped streaming with tears of regret, remorse and pangs of discord.

Soon life and order gave way to chaos and the streets could no longer be safe for play.

Mean and brutal, unforgiving and unjust cruel unthinkable acts happened from opening to dusk. Not a light in the sky, not a glimmer of hope. Pure deep darkness set in the city sky like a storm. It rained night and day yet not a raindrop would fall. But something was coming down no one could see what it was. The fall.

Back from the escort in six months' time, the Son returned to see. A cast of valleys and death on the horizon as he approached. It startled and shook him and would have snatched the very breath of life away. But he closed his eyes and rode forth till day. Upon entering the castle he called for his sister to come. But there was no voice. Only silence.

Not a usual beat of a drum upon the door but a knock. To his surprise, the warlords and beasts of men who rule the city did plan. They came to address him and give him his orders of his place in their land.

Quick did he see they were blind as bats so he leapt to his feet and danced on their laps. To the roof he would go and lay light upon the land and search to see where his sister might stand. From the north to the south, east, and west his light awakened the land beneath. And the warm glow of life brought death and darkness to its knees. It did not take long for all to be restored, but his heart was broken for his sister was no more.

He sent word to the King of this terrible report and the King though spent made the trip home in a night. A thief had come and stolen their most valued possession. His daughter, a sister, one day a beautiful queen.

A proper funeral was given. Though the casket was empty. A hole was dug and there placed inside, all the hopes and visions, all the dreams and all the legends.

She was lost.

Through struggling and wrestling she never could free, she did remember the secrets her father, the King did speak: "The voices of a stranger do not follow my child. But listen to me.

"Follow my voice. Whisper my name wherever you are and I will come and find you.

"Whisper my name."

"Did he mean when I failed him?

"Would his promise still find me?

"Tied to this tree I could not bear for Him to see me.

"To see my vain imaginings."

So she tried herself to free her wrists. Unlock the cuffs. *Fly open, you locks.*

Her hair grew long. Down the trunk of the tree it wrapped itself and fled to the soil.

She could no longer remember the sight she once stole of herself that fateful eve.

Like shutters and curtains she could faint remember what lay outside the windows of her grief. Filled with cobwebs and bats her thoughts no longer imagined or saw anything. Or anyone. She had at last forgotten all, foremost herself.

Lost was she.

The resigned tree held her repose as it lifted her frame as it grew to the sky. Her dress now mere shards of fabric grafted to the trunk, her dress changed colors in the cold autumn breeze. She was cursed as she hung on the tree. Guilty as shone. Deserving she exchanged all for this home.

With the turning of the leaves and their passing away, time flew quickly.

The King sent searchers to announce and explore the far regions of the Kingdom for her long lost soul. Calling into the night the King was hoarse every break of day from the weeping and speaking her name until He was broken. Heart torn apart from the endless seeking of a soul that was lost. No place too far. No expense not paid. He was desperate and would give anything, anybody in exchange.

Now where the sand did end and the waters began a kingdom not of His throne. Did a head not bow. This world of wilderness of wanderings of wicked men and world who

In a time before determined their destination was to not be HIS OWN. This place He could not enter nor search nor intervene for a law had been broken and they were separated by decree. Somewhere in the deep recesses of the King's open heart he knew his daughter to be there. Still by her own choice and fate was enough, his love and his grace could never stop. The yearning. Whispers. Messengers. Calling. Reaching.

The King had a plan.

The Son did not look back for a glance to the King for He knew the task ahead was for him to complete.

Through forests of ages and lands of pages, through trails of scrolls and paths foretold the King's Son passed through every one. He would not be hindered.

"He was bruised for my transgression, the chastisement of my peace fell upon Him and by His stripes I am healed."*

"Like a sheep before her shearers is dumb."*

"The wolves of Bashan."*

"For he humbled Himself."*

The words took form as the wind and blew Him forth.

At the fullness of day The Son came down from his steed and walked upon the cursed land.

There marking its entrance stood a tree. His sister now so intertwined he did not see.

The blinded heartless beggars heaped insults and ordered his feet upon their land to halt. But a child abused and neglected ran carefree. Leaping to his arms.

While kissing her gently on the head he did not see the hordes of humans running toward him. With jagged shards of glass their hands gripped forcefully. Relentlessly stabbing, dragging him back to the tree. They hoisted him up, stripped his body of its clothes and with fragments of glass nailed him to the tree. Though with every piercing a deeper light burst forth and blood flowed and freely coursed. The skies did open and water poured forth.

Blood and water. Darkness covered the land. An earthquake.

Then far deeper than any tree root could ever explore. The graves of millions did open. The light was unstoppable. It cured the whole earth. The tree split open and lifted its curse.

Dropped from her handcuffs and her bonds to the tree the daughter from captivity was immediately freed.

The Son shone down from the sky above. Standing beside Him was the Father of love.

He had found her at last. His soul now at peace. His love had rest. His heart now leaped for joy. Singing once again His song rang loud so all that desired to be free could walk into light from this moment on.

She was free.

As so as the pages of life upon the books of eternity do turn, there remain the questions.

Are you lost?
What has captured your eyes?
What have you pursued wandering far and beyond?

Are you chained to a tree?

There's hope.
The Father has searched for you for all your life.
The Son of God has come to seek and save the lost.

*see endnotes

A Word of Encouragement: Faithful and True

§

THERE ONCE WAS AN OLD horse that stood at the opening of his stall every day waiting for his rider to come. He stood motionless. Big, bare, broad back with daunting leg muscles and bushy mane and tail that hinted of a shadow of a previous glory ride.

This ride had been brief, but the rider tall and gentle whispered many words as they journeyed through the countryside. At last the ride ended, the rider walked on as the evening sun disappeared into the sky. His last words, *Wait for me. I will come to ride.*

Through many seasons, the horse stood alone. Fall turned to winter. Leaves falling to the earth as dew on the countryside grew to frost then daffodils, and at last the parched hot land felt cool again. Around and around the rains fell, bringing new seasons to the soil. But the horse kept waiting, seemingly stalled in time.

As moons went around other mares and stallions came. Passers-by. Running fast and free they marveled at the horse. Ungroomed, lackluster, it was becoming only a shadow of its youth.

They pleaded with the horse. But the horse replied, "I'm waiting for my rider."

"Silly, you've gone mad. Your rider has long forgotten you. Come rid yourself of this vigil. Break and run free with us while you can still run wild.

There's so much you haven't seen."

But the horse simply bowed his head, turned, and went down back into the stable.

This continued for many years until their season ended and they ceased to come.

Late one cloudy afternoon, though uneventful as always, the old horse looked out the opening of his stall to see a vaguely familiar figure. With its eyes nearly blind, its mane sparse and dry, it grunted and moved its awkward head.

The voice of the rider spoke faintly, not more than a whisper: "You have been faithful and true. Come now, I will ride."

His voice like lightning quickened the old weary bones, brightened the dim eyes; with passion and flame with a mane set on fire, he leaped over the stall, stood up on hind legs, and let out a roar.

Gone were the years of waiting. It seemed like only a day.
The rider was here.
The Mighty One now dwells among us. He rides on the wings of the wind.
*His glory and his joy surround us. As we exalt His majesty He reigns.**
The rider has come.
There are some who have waited for a very long time.
It is time to ride.

For more information on Deliver, please visit www.shellegraves.com

Journal notes

Made in the USA
Middletown, DE
24 October 2015